Just Trust Me

JUST TRUST ME

FINDING THE
TRUTH
IN A WORLD OF
SPIN

G. RANDY KASTEN

QUEST
BOOKS

Theosophical Publishing House
Wheaton, Illinois * Chennai, India

Quest Books
Theosophical Publishing House
P. O. Box 270
Wheaton, IL 60187-0270

www.questbooks.net

Cover design by Drew Stevens
Typesetting by Wordstop Technologies, Chennai, India

Library of Congress Cataloging-in-Publication Data

Kasten, G. Randy.
Just trust me: finding the truth in a world of spin / G. Randy Kasten.—1st Quest ed.
      p.   cm.
Includes index.
ISBN 978-0-8356-0889-3
1. Truthfulness and falsehood. 2. Truth. 3. Reality. I. Title.
BJ1421.K37 2011
177'.3—dc22   2011013121

5   4   3   2   1   *   11   12   13   14   15

Printed in the United States of America

For Helene, who understood.

Contents

Preface

I have been asked how I came to write a book about truth. The seeds were planted by an experience I had at age fifteen. It was 1970, and my family had recently moved from the San Francisco Bay Area to a town in the San Joaquin Valley. I was a teenager anxious to fit in. To say that I was going through culture shock would be an understatement. Especially at the time, the social climate in the Bay Area was liberal and tolerant, while in the San Joaquin Valley that was not the case. On my first day of school there, the P.E. teacher took my name down and asked, "That an Okie name?" After four students were shot and killed at a Kent State Vietnam War protest, a kid I knew said, "Just shoot a few of 'em. That'll put a stop to it." He was being serious, not sarcastic.

One evening I found myself sitting on a couch at my friend Earl's house, watching a color TV housed in a large wooden console. Walter Cronkite was finishing up a newscast with a bit of commentary. He spoke about the dangers of making up one's mind too quickly and labeling events before fully understanding them. Cronkite urged his viewers to use restraint and think carefully. His concluding phrase was something like, "Let's not be too quick to use the label-making device."

Earl looked over at me. "Do you know what the crap he was talking about?"

"Hell, no," I drawled. "Why do they put that kinda stuff on TV, anyway?"

Earl just shook his head.

I did not have the courage to tell Earl that Walter Cronkite was a distant relative, nor to let on that I thought I understood what Cronkite was saying.

Soon after, Walter Cronkite was voted the most trusted man in America.

Years later, I realized that even if I had understood Cronkite, I had failed to follow his advice. I had attached too many labels and made too many assumptions.

This book describes how we can remove the label-making device and see through deceptions of all types. We value what we know is true. Some are amused by the cleverness of their own lies, but most of us find little worth in what we suspect is false. The deceptions that surround us are temporary and hollow. They give us nothing of lasting value.

While many of the thoughts expressed in this book are my own, any genuine wisdom you may find has come to me from other people; the only credit I can take is for having a good memory. I owe a tremendous debt to those who shared their thoughts with me in conversations and letters, some of them decades ago, and I owe even more to the people who helped me develop the book itself. I have attempted to faithfully reflect their insight and intelligence. Any failure to express clearly what they have taught me is my own.

While nothing in the book should be taken as legal advice for any specific situation, I hope my insights will be useful to you on many occasions.

Acknowledgments

Many people have contributed to this book, directly and indirectly. The tremendous amount of support others have provided is difficult to quantify and its value too easy to underestimate.

I would like to thank the many fine teachers and professors I have had, including particularly Diane Bernard, Tom Swope, John Faggi, Ken Grantham, Caroline Kerr Gage, and the late William Dickey and James Crumley. I also learned a great deal about writing from Rob Garros, Doug Hiney, Michele French, Roxanne Barber, Mike Shaler, Kathy Briccetti, and Dean Bernal. For their support and encouragement, my appreciation to Bill Haskell, Toby Goddard, Julia Scheeres, David Moltzen, Edie Meidav, and, of course, my father, George Kasten, sister Sandy, son Will, and niece Corina.

For their patient reading, contributions of ideas, and editorial assistance, I would particularly like to thank Blair Kilpatrick, Walter Rimler, Margit Stange, Rachel Zauer, and Radhika Mathur.

My sincere gratitude to Mike Larsen and Elizabeth Pomada for their support, agenting, and generous contributions of ideas. Sharron Dorr, publishing manager of Quest Books, has been a pleasure to work with, as has my editor, Judith Stein. Thanks to Dr. Bram Fridhandler, who provided input on psychological topics; Doug Perednia, M.D., and Eva Hersh, M.D., also provided valuable facts. Terry Murphey helped with historical information, and Beth La Vigne Swanburg generously shared her thoughts on social and political topics. For their assistance with the chapter on science, my appreciation to Bo Curry and Alex Madonik. I am indebted to Rutie Adler and Eve Sweetser of the University of California, Berkeley, for their help with cognitive science, social issues, and linguistics. To those people who provided valuable insights about the truth but understandably asked not to be publicly identified, thank you for your candor.

Above all, I thank my wife, Helene Maxwell, for her untiring support, her assistance with research and proofreading, and her limitless insights about the truth.

Introduction

I am an attorney who has been practicing civil litigation for more than twenty-five years. Much of *Just Trust Me* is the result of hearing thousands of lies. Seeing patterns in why lies were told and how they were structured, I wanted to write a useful book that would help people uncover the facts. This book provides methods for finding the truth in daily situations.

What we regard as true shapes our beliefs, attitudes, and actions. Our definition of what is true affects what happens to us and what occurs in society. Yet we can believe things that have no basis in fact. People are capable of embracing horrific precepts that seem incredible in retrospect. In Nazi Germany, Adolf Hitler had millions of followers who accepted his ideas. Principles of racial superiority were widely accepted as the truth, and those who did not accept them could not speak freely. As Voltaire put it long before Hitler's time, "Those who can make you believe absurdities can make you commit atrocities."

The illusions we are offered in everyday life are more subtle, but they affect us directly and personally. Some illusions, such as films and novels, we seek out and appreciate. Other illusions can make us miserable and even kill us. For example, we need to know if particular foods that taste perfectly fine can hurt us in the short term (as with *Salmonella* contamination) or in the long term (cholesterol), whether a prevalent virus is so dangerous we should avoid public places, and what problems a local political candidate may cause or resolve if elected. We want to know if items we purchase are durable or junk and whether people we are attracted to are truly as considerate as they seem at first. Being able to see quickly beyond surface appearances allows us to have more prosperity, better health, and greater intimacy.

But gaining those insights can be a challenge. As economic problems and political campaigns illustrate, we are surrounded by illusions, some of them deliberately created. This book demonstrates how false impressions can work their way into our belief systems. For example:

We believe stories because they are the ones available. Most people would identify Thomas Edison as the inventor of the incandescent light bulb, but that is not the case. Although Edison perfected a commercially successful design, he was preceded in the experimentation by British inventors Frederick de Moleyns and Joseph Swan and by American J. W. Starr.[1]

Beliefs may justify past actions. In July 2006, half the respondents to a Harris Poll said they believed that when the United States invaded in March 2003, Iraq possessed weapons of mass destruction.[2] But in 2004, the CIA had concluded that Iraq had no stockpiles of illicit weapons.

We may not recognize the significance of our own perceptions. In November 2005, a suicide bomber struck the Radisson Hotel in Amman, Jordan. On the eighth floor, Ita Martin was in her room. Although she heard a loud noise, it was not until she turned on CNN that she realized what the noise had been. "Oh, my God, I'm in that hotel," she exclaimed.[3]

This book demonstrates why the biggest enemies of truth are the people whose job it is to sell us incomplete versions of the available facts; our willingness to believe what we want to believe; and the simple absence of accurate information.

In business and social interactions, people constantly offer us selective presentations of the truth. Companies advertising products on television do not describe the advantages of their competitors' products any more than a man asking a woman to marry him encourages her to date other men before making up her mind. It is a social reality that people encourage one another to make important decisions with limited groups of facts.

Technology has both simplified and complicated the fact-gathering process. While the Internet provides resources that makes it possible to check facts more easily, it also disburses misinformation. Technology delivers more convincing illusions, such as in films and digitally altered photographs. Today, we are particularly susceptible to manipulation by advertisers, salespeople, politicians, and the media. Technology has made it easier for those who control access to information to dazzle us with a modern version of smoke and mirrors. Slanted versions of facts increasingly champion technique over content.

Yet the cost of decisions based on unfounded beliefs can be high. For years, many people subscribed to the mistaken belief that because sport utility vehicles (SUVs) were large, they were also necessarily safer than other vehicles in all respects. However, single-vehicle rollovers cause more fatalities than any other type of accident. Sixty-three percent of all SUV deaths in 1999 were from rollovers. In 2000, SUVs had the highest rollover rate (36 percent) of any vehicle type involved in fatal accidents. Yet in 2002, one out of four vehicles being sold in the United States was an SUV.[4] The myth of SUV safety persisted even as statistics mounted that SUVs were unsafe and before safety improvements seriously addressed the problem.

The essential question we face over and over again in a typical day is, "How do I know this is true?" This book shows you how to apply the following questions:

- Is the information complete enough on which to base a decision, or are important facts missing?
- Is the information source you are consulting inherently biased?
- Are you distorting the available information yourself?
- What information is the most important to have?

The book also considers when it is most important to have our guard up. By understanding human nature, we can know when deception is most likely to occur. We lie when we feel inadequate, afraid, or guilty. We lie when we think we will not be believed if we tell the truth. We speak untruths out of habit, to protect others, and when our emotions conflict. We lie to ourselves when the truth or the unknown are unacceptable. We lie about how we feel when we believe the truth would be unacceptable to others.

We want to be loved and understood for who we are. We may present a persona to the world that is different from how we feel, one we believe will bring respect and acceptance. Ironically, we are then valued for our ability to play a role, not for who we are. You can help other people who face that dilemma to be more honest with you by accepting the flaws they find unacceptable in themselves. The book shows you other specific ways to build trust and promote honest communication.

We can also be fooled because we see ourselves as reasonably intelligent people who know what is real. We maintain our self-image partly by not asking "stupid" questions that might actually help us get at the truth. Manipulators can take advantage of our desire to project confidence, indirectly assuring us we are too smart to need explanations.

This book is about more than outright lies. It is also about rejecting false notions that are destructive and that may cause us to respond harshly to those who deserve our empathy. For example, misogynist beliefs may lead to a rape victim being blamed for the crime: "She brought it on herself by dressing that way." Or a wife who is abused may be seen as complicit in the abuse: "Why didn't she just leave?" When a factory shuts down and a man is laid off from the job he held for twenty years, he may be regarded as a loser. If we incorporate false ideas into our ways of thinking, our mental models will be incomplete and inaccurate. We will be less able to understand what is necessary to create change in our lives or even to see when change is desirable.

The discussion explores how we have to work hard, although sometimes unconsciously, to maintain accurate perceptions. For example, patients in the intensive care unit (ICU) of a hospital may develop a condition known as ICU psychosis.[5] When placed in ICU, patients who were previously mentally healthy may become excited, anxious, paranoid, delusional and exhibit other symptoms of cognitive distress. Numerous medical causes can play a role, including the effects of disease, medications, sleeplessness, infections, or low blood-oxygen levels. But a major factor is believed to be sensory deprivation.[6] In an ICU, there are continuous light levels that do not allow distinction between night and day. Contact with family and friends may be limited. Patients in an ICU are especially prone to feel helpless. Some estimates are that a third of patients will have some form of ICU psychosis after five days, although the psychosis usually resolves once the patient is released. The prevalence of the condition and the tendency to recover after release suggest how vulnerable we all are to losing our bearings when familiar cues are removed. This also suggests we do mental work, consciously or not, to remain oriented throughout the day. To see the world with great clarity, conscious effort is certainly necessary.

There are significant challenges to maintaining an accurate and comprehensive mental model of the world, and of course no one does it perfectly. When we are with other people, we benefit from their accurate perceptions, but the vast majority of our interpretations of the world are made alone. It is a constant process. We reset the hour, day, month, season, and year in our heads as often as necessary. We note where we are physically, and we usually have an accurate sense of what is likely to transpire over the course of the next few hours and even over the next few days. Much is automatic; going through the day is a bit like driving a car—we do not need to know what each moving part is doing at all times. We deal with the bigger picture of applying the brakes at appropriate times, steering around obstacles, and keeping gas in the tank. Yet the more information we have, the better we can plan. If we know the fuel pump is about to fail, we will not rely on the car. If we know there is construction work or an accident along the route, we will go another way. Sometimes we do not know about the fuel pump or the traffic delay. Sometimes other people take down road signs or put up fake signs to confuse us.

It is as though we have to constantly recognize pictures made from jigsaw puzzle pieces, but with many of the pieces missing. Life compels us to put incomplete clues together, grasp the general idea, and make quick decisions in the situations we encounter. Every specific fact we can add to our general knowledge will allow us to recognize the overall picture more quickly and sharply and thus avoid making mistakes.

We design our own futures, protect ourselves and our families from dangers, and provide ourselves with what brings us happiness. Without accurate information on which to base decisions, our success is going to be limited. We can be our own worst enemy at times by resisting new and accurate information. Whether we have good information, no information at all, distorted information from salespeople, limited role models, or irresponsible opinions from media personalities who are rewarded for being outrageous, we are still the ones who must ultimately decide what is real.

To talk about the truth further, we need to establish what the word means. This requires a stroll into the esoteric field of philosophy, much of which is written in obscure language by authors who did not try very hard to connect with their readers. The excursion will be brief.

Although we all have a working definition of the word *truth*, it is best described as a constellation of concepts rather than a single one. Different contexts call for different definitions.

Objective truths are the provable facts most people would agree on— for instance, that the earth revolves around the sun. Importantly, not everything we regard as being beyond argument today always has been. Even the most reliable facts are not necessarily more than highly reliable patterns; even reliable patterns may be subject to exception.

Subjective truths, more accurately labeled as beliefs, are concepts that are true for the speaker. They are frequently confused with objective truths, or the concepts that are true for everyone. For example, someone might say, "That person is really ugly." If you were to point out that ugliness is a subjective judgment, the speaker would almost certainly respond, "Come on. Just about anybody would say he's ugly"—as though anticipated consensus makes a subjective opinion objectively true. When we label subjective beliefs as objective truths, problems may arise, such as racism ("Those people are inferior"), entitlement ("The rules don't apply to me because . . .") and distorted thinking ("I just feel lucky/unlucky"). This mislabeling can cause people to twist their interpretations around until the subjective belief takes on the appearance of objective truth. Sometimes other people are enlisted to agree that a subjective belief is actually an objective truth and may be rewarded for agreeing:

"You're right, it *is* true—I never thought of it that way."

"No wonder I like you so much!"

Yet despite their highly personal nature, and probably because of it, subjective truths can seem even *more* certain than objective truths. In 2005, comedian Stephen Colbert began playing with the absurdity of subjective truth by using the term *truthiness*.[7]

Relative truths have a greater degree of truth than some other premises. A dark shade of red, for example, may be a purer red than a shade that tends more toward orange, while both could still accurately be called "red." An example in economic terms is how we accept that homeowner's or renter's insurance premiums may be expensive, but that in relation to a catastrophic loss from a fire, the premiums are a bargain.

Probable truths are concepts that are more likely true than not. Your neighbor may say, "My car runs," because it usually does, then go out into his driveway to discover it will not start. His statement was only a probable truth.

Potential truths are those that might be so, but that are not necessarily so. As with other beliefs, potential truths may become confused with objective truths. That one can vividly imagine winning the lottery does not make it more likely to happen. Nor will worrying about contracting an obscure disease make coming down with it more probable. Potential truths are possible given the right conditions, but that is all.

Consensus truths are the taboos, laws, and rules of etiquette we agree on. They are not truths in any tangible sense; they are subjective beliefs to which we collectively give the same credence we give to objective truths.

Temporary truths are concepts that are reliable one day but not another. "Peaches are in season here" may be a true statement if made in July but not if made in January.

Contextual truths are beliefs that are true only within a certain framework. "I'm the smartest person in the room" is true consistently only if one is careful about which rooms one goes into.

Implied truths are truths suggested by groupings of ideas or truths that involve comparisons. A small house pictured among much larger houses seems to be worth more than a small house surrounded by other small houses. Implied truths are often created by putting the target concept next to a second concept that has no logical connection to the first. But because the second is emotionally loaded, its impact seeps into the target concept.

People have asked me if I think the truth even exists. While I believe it does, each of the definitions of *truth*, including objective truth, may more accurately be called a belief. Some are more reliable than others, but ultimately we are all stuck inside ourselves, coming close to seeing the truth but never having a complete picture.

Some may find the process of examining the amounts of misinformation we are exposed to, the process of turning over so many rocks, discouraging or disturbing. Please understand that my intent is to encourage skepticism, not cynicism or pessimism. The difference is significant. No one wants to be taken advantage of, have decisions made for him, or be treated like a fool. There is a great deal we can do to slow and even stop the spin we are handed. I have tried to present the material in a way that emphasizes the benefits of accurate perceptions and helps the reader avoid practical mistakes. The emphasis is on critical thinking. Where it seemed useful to make a specific suggestion, I have indicated that with an arrow →. Some of the points I make may seem obvious, but what is obvious to some readers may not be obvious to all. Each of us sees the world a little differently.

Just Trust Me explores truth in the environments we encounter in daily life, and the description of each context is necessarily brief.

Entire books have been written on each of the topics mentioned in this one; I have tried to capture enough of their essence to generate discussion.

I have also attempted to make it clear when I am merely stating my personal opinion. You may not agree with all my observations. I encourage you to reconsider those you reject and to question those you agree with. In short, *do not* trust me, and do not trust yourself. If there is a central message in this book, it is that all our beliefs are worth a second look.

1

←——————→

Just Trust Me

Only other people get tricked.

Certainly not lawyers, professionals who spend most of their time being suspicious, asking questions, and revealing the truth. Imagine my surprise when I learned that the office manager of a law firm where I worked had been embezzling money from us for more than three years.

How did we allow this to happen? While her accounting tricks were not sophisticated, she worked the human angle flawlessly. She knew that many good lawyers are not good business people. We prefer to do what we are best at—practicing law—rather than doing accounting, filling out forms, or shopping for affordable health-insurance plans. We trusted her because she did all those things and did them well. She was friendly and upbeat; she made it easy to trust her.

Being an attorney, especially in a litigation firm, means being constantly on guard; some lawyers will pull a fast one if they can. Yet as much as constant suspicion is part of a lawyer's job, it is tiring and unpleasant to question everyone all the time. Just as none of us wanted to carry our skepticism home and cross-examine our spouses, none of us wanted to be suspicious of someone in our own office. We saw our office manager every day. Outwardly, she was a cheerful, politically conservative woman who taught Sunday school. She was attractive and dressed nicely. At work, she seemed to look out for everyone else's interests. Except for the embezzlement, I have to say she did her job very well. Two-signature checks and periodic audits seemed unnecessary. It did not help that we were a bunch of confident lawyers who thought we knew everything, were infallibly able to recognize deception, and were sure that if there were a crook among us, we would see it in an instant. We thought we *knew* our office manager was trustworthy.

The difference between our subjective belief and the objective truth turned out to be extreme. If she had seemed unfriendly and had grumbled about how little she was being paid, it would have been easier to suspect her of a crime. As it turned out, our supposed knowledge was nothing more than conjecture and a collection of false impressions. The attorneys I worked with were all smart people and fine lawyers, but that was not enough to allow us to see what was under our noses.

Mainly because of financial pressures, the law firm split in two. Shortly afterward, an attorney at one of the new firms (the one where the office manager had gone to work) noticed an unusually large expenditure. Now less willing to assume there was nothing to investigate, the attorney started going through the books. It did not take her long to realize that many of the entries in the check register were faked. Checks ostensibly made out for office supplies and law library books had actually been written to the office manager herself or to pay off her credit cards. Entries in the register, made to look like carbons of what was written on the checks, all reflected legitimate-looking expenses. Records from the original law firm were examined; those books had been faked as well. The processed checks told the real story, but our office manager had known when to expect their arrival in the mail along with the bank statements every month. In hindsight, we realized she had always made sure to be there to open the mail when it mattered, even planning her vacations around the date.

After we called the police, the office manager was arrested and prosecuted. Among other repercussions, some twenty people who had worked with her needed to come to grips with the experience of being completely wrong about her character. Everyone had the same initial reaction: if they had been asked to make a list of everyone who worked for the original firm in the order of people most-to-least likely to embezzle, the office manager would have been at the very bottom of their list.

Their other reactions differed in interesting ways. Some took a simple view: The office manager was a bad person, and they had been victimized. The people who saw themselves as victims did not pause to consider that their blind trust had been a mistake. Other people, alarmed by the lack of common sense, became convinced that she had taken more money than we could trace. Some even began imagining a suitcase full of cash, perhaps buried overseas.

The embezzlement affected the profitability and survival of the original firm. Even though our office manager's actions reduced my compensation, I was more curious about what had gone on inside her head than I was angry. As the attorney who attended the criminal hearings and prosecuted a civil case against her on behalf of one of the two successor law firms, I was in a good position to satisfy my curiosity. From everything she had done and everything she eventually admitted, it seemed that she had been able to keep her criminal actions separated not only from her public personality but from the rest of her consciousness. To the extent she remained aware of her bad side, she justified her actions, believing she should have been paid more. We had believed she was someone other than who she really was, and for the most part, she believed she was too.

Flying Blind

One of the more publicized incidents attributed to the legend of the Bermuda Triangle involved five Navy airplanes that left Fort Lauderdale, Florida, just after 2:00 p.m. on December 5, 1945, and never returned. This was Flight 19, a training mission led by Lt. Charles Taylor.[1] After flying out to sea, Lt. Taylor saw a string of islands below and became convinced he had mistakenly flown south over the Florida Keys instead of east over the Atlantic as intended. He concluded that his compasses were not working and that the way home was a path generally north.

His route then took him and his student pilots even farther out over the Atlantic Ocean.

Intercepted radio transmissions indicated that the students were questioning his navigation, but Lt. Taylor ignored them as well as efforts radioed from the mainland to guide the planes back to land. The planes would have exhausted their fuel by 8:00 p.m. that evening and are presumed to have made forced landings in the sea, where they quickly sank. The flight leader had discarded multiple pieces of information and insisted on sticking with a belief that cost all the aviators their lives.

There were other interesting aspects to the tragedy, although these were not as widely discussed. Separate mistaken impressions had also formed in the minds of the four pilots under Lt. Taylor's command. While they questioned his judgment and knew it was suicidal to fly farther out to sea at night in bad weather until their fuel was exhausted, they still followed their leader to their deaths. Instead of breaking out of formation and following their own compass headings back to a safe landing in Florida, the student pilots remained convinced that the most important thing of all was to follow orders. These pilots were not in combat; they were not sacrificing themselves for a greater good. Nothing critical depended on their blind obedience to the orders of a confused and probably panicked commanding officer. Preserving themselves and the planes they flew could only have helped the Navy. Yet their military training had convinced them that the appropriate response was to give a higher priority to following orders than to their own survival.

One other lesson may be taken from Flight 19: strong emotions can breed misinformation. Not only was Lt. Taylor too stubborn or proud to accept a radioed offer from one of the student pilots to guide the group back to land, but his mother later petitioned the Navy to change its original report about the incident. She succeeded, and the loss of Flight 19 was mysteriously attributed to "causes or reasons unknown." This obscured the facts of the incident and encouraged public speculation about the existence of an area that became labeled the "Bermuda Triangle." Although some still insist that the Bermuda Triangle contains mysterious forces, that idea is now widely believed to be a myth, with no more losses of ships and planes than any other comparably sized patch of ocean.

Making good decisions involves not only having information but evaluating the integrity of the information, such as whether a compass is malfunctioning. Good decisions also require one to decide which pieces of information to pay attention to. The Navy pilots were guided not only by compasses but by visual cues from island formations and the position of the sun before it set, radio transmissions from the mainland, their clocks and fuel gauges, and one anothers' perceptions. Lt. Taylor paid attention only to a mistaken visual cue, while his students paid the most attention to the concept of following orders. At our law office, we paid the most attention to a woman's demeanor, lifestyle, appearance, and apparent competence. We liked the pleasant illusion she presented; our desire to believe in it distracted us from the truth. Neither the Navy pilots nor the lawyers sought out and paid attention to the most important clues.

Blind Justice

Different disciplines have their own methods for finding the truth. Criminal and civil trials are designed to bring out the truth within a highly structured setting. Some facts are allowed by the judge to be presented and considered as relevant evidence, while others—although they might have a loose connection to the questions to be decided— are not. For example, a jury is not allowed to know everything about a person accused of robbing a bank. They will not hear that he is a Republican or a Democrat. They will not learn whether he is a Baptist, an Episcopalian, or an atheist. His political and religious beliefs are not linked to the question of whether he robbed the bank, and those details might make jurors like or dislike the accused. Jurors could be more or less willing to convict for a reason unrelated to the crime. They might, in other words, *pay attention to the wrong cue.*

As explained in detail in chapter 3, our legal system does not trust jurors' ability to ignore distractions, especially emotionally charged ones. The system acknowledges that when people are asked to make decisions, they may have difficulty picking out the most telling facts. They may have trouble distinguishing their own feelings and personal experiences from the focused questions a trial is meant to resolve. As they hear objections from the attorneys being sustained by the judge just as a particularly juicy fact is about to be presented, or when they are told to disregard certain evidence, some jurors resent the implied lack of trust in their judgment. They want to hear everything. Since they trust themselves not to be biased, why shouldn't the court? Who does not want to believe he or she is wise enough to recognize what is important, sort out distractions, and reject attempts at distortion or deception? After all, feelings and personal experiences are exactly what allow all of us to draw conclusions and make decisions in our own lives.

Centuries of experience tell us people cannot be counted on to see everything objectively. Different people will arrive at different conclusions based on the same evidence. People have prejudices and passions that may mean far more to them than cold, objective facts. Because the decisions of jurors affect other people, courts strive for as much objectivity as possible. Potential jurors are probed for feelings, experiences, and beliefs that could be strong enough to obscure a rational interpretation of the evidence.

Lawyers, incidentally, have no problem with jurors who are inclined to pay the most attention to clues that will favor their client. Lawyers are not looking for unprejudiced jurors; they are looking for jurors with prejudices they like. People are influenced by the wrong clues all the time, and lawyers, advertisers, and persuaders of all types use that tendency to their advantage whenever they can. It is the judge who acts as a filter throughout a trial, keeping, or trying to keep, evidence away from the jury that might distract its members from the narrow factual questions to be decided. Even with the scope of the evidence limited by a judge, people will still disagree about how much attention to give a fact. Before reaching a verdict, juries will consider the relative weight of the evidence. A robbery suspect may have been identified in part because he was seen wearing a blue shirt. Given the probable number of people wearing blue shirts that day, the shirt alone does not support a conviction. However, a surveillance video showing the face of a man who strongly resembles the robber will be given a lot more weight than the color of his shirt. If collecting clues and arriving at the truth is like assembling the pieces of a jigsaw puzzle, a strong clue such as the video is a corner piece.

Life rarely hands us such obvious signs. Most of the puzzle pieces go somewhere in the middle, and we spend most of our time sorting them out. We have to interpret subtle hints and constantly collect and weigh small bits of information. Because we live in an age of images manufactured and manipulated by technology, the challenges of paying attention to the right clues and deciding what weight to give them is even harder. Technology can also create a sense of urgency that demands rushed decisions: a fax or an e-mail message can seem more urgent than a letter arriving in the mail. Electronic devices and mass media bring us more information from which to select. We need effective methods for deciding what is true, especially in fields in which we are not expert. We need ways to conduct our own trials, to sort nonsense from substance.

Truth is not always self-evident; often we must deliberately seek it out. For example, you may find it convenient or comforting to put complete trust in others—your doctor, your lawyer, a member of the clergy, your office manager, or your flight leader—then blame that person if the truth he or she presents turns out to be wrong. The better alternative is to gather information from multiple sources and then have the courage to act on the information.

→ One method you can try is this:

Imagine that you are looking at the world from your perspective, but with a wide-angle lens. Your wide-angle lens sees the big picture. This lens sees not only the way a person intends to present himself to you but also what he does not intend to present. If you are on a date, you can catch glimpses not just of the person your date wants you to believe he or she is but of who he or she really is, by observing:

- How does she treat the waiter? Is she polite, curt, timid?
- If a dish on the menu is unavailable, does he pout or just make another selection?
- Does he admit having faults or talk only about his strengths?
- Is she curious about her surroundings or more interested in showing off what she already knows?

By paying attention to the wide picture, you will see beyond what people say and how they say it. Their deliberate presentations are important, but they are also the most obvious and often the most distorted. You can look more widely and also observe what makes someone happy and what their needs and eccentricities are. It is easy to become distracted by what someone *wants* us to see. When you look for the broader context of how a person interacts with the world, you will come a lot closer to understanding who he or she is.

The complementary method is:

Imagine standing outside the situation, looking at yourself objectively. You may see how you want to believe your date is going to be clever, generous, and fun—not only today, but forever. After all, when you invest your time in someone, you may prefer to think you are out with a person with great qualities and are receiving the attention and respect of someone desirable. You may fall for an act largely because you want to believe your date is always that charming and attentive, even though you cannot know how he or she is going to act six weeks or six years from now. Yet as with classic con games, you can be convinced to go along with something too good to be true only if you get excited enough not to carefully examine what is offered. It is not romantic, but understanding what you want to see, and what you are personally most inclined to overlook, is a lot better than ending up in a bad relationship. If you can envision yourself from a distance, you can see the temptations you face and your vulnerabilities in the situation.

→ The next time you see a TV commercial for a car, watch how you react to images of attractive people in the ad as they listen to magnificent music and experience the best of all life has to offer:

- Does some tiny part of you want to believe that the car comes with miles of beautiful, open roads to enjoy instead of the ugly, traffic-clogged highways you really drive on?
- Does it influence you just a little if the driver has a good-looking companion in the passenger seat?
- Do you believe that strangers are actually going to turn their heads in admiration as you drive past?
- Does a part of you want to go along with the sale of the sizzle, even when you know all that is really for sale is a mobile collection of metal, glass, and plastic?
- Can you, sitting over there on the couch, imagine just the car *without* the people in it, without the background scenery and music?

→ If, on the other hand, you are reading a newspaper article, your wide-angle lens can question the source:

- Was the reporter there when the event happened, or did she piece the story together afterward?
- Is there an interview with just one or with half a dozen witnesses to the event?
- Do the comments of the eyewitnesses show them blurting out their emotional reactions as a personal catharsis, or are they making an effort to describe the event so others can understand?

- Have witnesses even had time to consider what they are saying?
- Are people giving their opinions or stating facts?
- If an opinion is given, how qualified is the person speaking? Does he have any specialized knowledge about the topic?

In nearly any situation, you can use your wide-angle lens to look at the source of the information coming at you and use your distance perspective so you can watch your own reactions.

→ Using the perspective of distance from yourself, you can also ask:

- Are you so experienced and confident in a situation that you are in danger of overlooking potential problems?
- Do you tell yourself that other people may have prejudices, but not you?
- Are there times when you are in danger of making bad decisions because of the mood you are in?
- Do you tell yourself your ego never plays a role in how you see things?
- Do you believe you never try to pretend you are a little more informed than you are?
- Do you ever assume the worst to avoid disappointment?
- Do you think you are smart enough to immediately see through any con?
- Do you believe that you never see only what you want to see?

Many of our thoughts and feelings are not admirable, so we hide them. Just as Lt. Taylor's mother was ashamed of her son's disorientation, and just as I felt shame when I wrote about our embezzling office manager, we can be tempted to rewrite history or offer justifications that hide realities. Fear may be disguised as prudence; greed may be labeled as ambition. A need for control can masquerade as organization. We present our best face to the world to keep our jobs and to maintain our reputations, self-image, and relationships. Daily, we paint over our worst qualities with our best. We offer certain illusions to other people and often to ourselves.

Illusions are often accepted at face value because of our need to categorize information quickly. You may have had the experience of seeing something strange in the sky, staring at the object until it fits into an existing frame of reference, such as an airplane from an unusual angle, a blimp, or a kite in the distance. Sometimes we do not know how to quickly put an odd thing into context, and that can be troubling. The most accurate conclusion in some situations may be the slightly uncomfortable realization that we *just do not know* the truth. Rather than accept uncertainty, we may quickly pigeonhole new information. Convenient explanations are reassuring and fit in with what we already know and believe. If we are to function well, we cannot be paralyzed by endless analysis and cannot afford to insist on detailed, verified facts about everything. Yet forming opinions based on the wrong clues or without reliable evidence invites bad decisions and limits opportunities. The relationship we have with information because of how we gather it, process it, and sometimes ignore it is a critical component of the effectiveness, satisfaction, and wisdom we will know in our lives.

Finding the Most Useful Truths

One salient truth may seem obvious to you in any given situation. A less obvious but more useful truth, however, may become apparent after a little thought. For example, you may recognize that someone will be motivated to do a task if you threaten to take away a benefit or privilege if the person fails to do it. This may be your first choice if you are feeling irritated, and you could stop there. But if you take a look at yourself, recognize your irritation, and also see the other person objectively, you may recognize that the same person is motivated to do the same task when you say you know you can count on them to do a good job. Either approach will result in the chore getting done, but one will produce a residue of resentment, while the other will leave the person happy to do more for you. Seeing the bigger picture and recognizing more than one truth will give you the power to make the best choice.

→ In the same way that judges and juries have a duty to understand the truth, you owe that duty to yourself. Every day, you make decisions that affect your life in large and small ways. Decisions based on the truth are far better decisions. More of the truth will emerge when you answer two questions:

- What is the *whole* picture?
- What do you *want* to see?

2

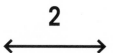

Eight Types of Lies and What You Can Do About Them

A study by University of Massachusetts psychologist Robert Feldman in 2002 determined that during a ten-minute conversation, 60 percent of people made at least one deliberate misrepresentation and, on average, told two or three lies.[1] Yet Feldman was examining only deliberate lies in conversations. Lies come in many other forms, so we are exposed to them even more than his study suggests. Despite the challenges, if you can recognize the *types* of lies that are most commonly told, you will see the underlying misrepresentations much more quickly.

Here are eight forms of lies, ranging from simple to complex.

Deliberate lies. When a person intentionally represents something to be different than what he believes or knows it to be, that is a deliberate lie. A child whose face is covered with cookie crumbs but denies taking a cookie is telling an outright lie. You already know that deliberate lies are most easily detected by fact checking and assessing a person's demeanor as they speak. Deliberate lies can also be signaled by any change in a person's usual behavior, such as talking faster or slower than what is normal for him. Lies make most people anxious, and the tension behind that anxiety is always looking for a way to express itself through behavior, like steam escaping through a small hole. There will be a whistle, a rattle, something out of place. Gratuitous, sometimes convoluted explanations frequently give people away. Watch for seemingly unnecessary explanations.

There is more information on detecting the deliberate lie in chapter 5.

Self-deception. A child who convinces himself he did not steal a cookie (maybe he only "borrowed" it) may speak with as much conviction as one who really did not. Unless cookie crumbs are visible, self-deception can be harder to detect, because the liar may not feel guilty or anxious. We sometimes sense when a person is in denial or deep into rationalization when his statements are a little too adamant.

Exaggerating. Exaggeration is the misrepresentation of quantities and/ or qualities. It can seem less objectionable than an outright lie because it amplifies or downplays facts, rather than creating or omitting them entirely; and the context often alerts the listener to protect herself. We know not to believe everything salespeople tell us, and we listen skeptically to politicians' speeches. As we get to know certain individuals, we may come to expect that they will exaggerate, and then discount everything they say as a countermeasure. Exaggeration is an accepted part of communication. Just about everyone does it at times; exaggeration is an easy way of making a situation seem more interesting or a fact more notable. It is also done when the speaker believes anything he says is going to be treated as exaggeration anyway, and he thinks he has to oversell.

Lying by omission. When a critical fact is left out of a presentation, listeners are pointed toward a false conclusion. If you are shopping for a computer, you reasonably expect to be told if its price does not include the monitor, keyboard, and mouse pictured in the advertisement. An appliance salesperson may be able to sell a refrigerator by talking about its aesthetic qualities and fantastic ice maker but failing to mention its mediocre energy efficiency and horrible repair record. The usual defense is, "You didn't ask!" Yet lies by omission are about things any reasonable person would have wanted to know—precisely the reason they were left out. We can protect ourselves by asking questions even, or especially, when they seem unnecessary.

White lies. Untruths are sometimes generated by unselfish motives. They may even be requested—for example, in the classic question, "Does this dress make me look fat?" White lies are more palatable than deliberate, selfish lies, because usually the intent is benign. If your mother is in the hospital recovering from a heart attack and asks about her miniature Schnauzer, it is probably not the best time to tell her the dog was hit by a car. We generally agree that sometimes it is best to misrepresent the truth.

On the other hand, lies labeled as white lies are sometimes told for self-serving reasons. For example, employees may leave negative facts out of a business presentation because they do not want to be a purveyor of bad news while telling themselves they do not want to upset the boss unnecessarily.

Intellectual dishonesty. Intellectual dishonesty is an attempt to mislead through fallacious reasoning. It can be perpetrated by people who consciously know better as well as by those who do not. Proponents may offer facts that are well documented but do not actually lead to the conclusion urged. For instance, a person who has money invested in the coal industry may point to an unusually cool summer or a series of heavy winter snowstorms to argue that global warming is nonsense and that therefore restrictions on burning coal are unnecessary. But this is misleading, because measurements reflecting global warming must be made on a vast scale over a long period if they are to accurately represent any trend. Although instances of colder-than-normal weather represent incidents rather than a trend, they may appear to be compelling evidence against global warming. For one thing, we experience weather on a personal, visceral level, whereas data illustrating the trend of global warming is abstract and impersonal, and it requires the layperson to put a great deal of faith in the scientific community. A sheet of ice on the sidewalk may be more persuasive than a sheet of paper filled with numbers, even though the former is entirely irrelevant to whether global warming is occurring.

When questions are lies. Questions can be lies if they pretend to convey curiosity, concern, or humor when there is an underlying motive. Suppose a man lends his son the family car for the evening and the next morning discovers a dent in the fender. He might say to his son, "I never noticed that dent before. Did you?" The man knows perfectly well the dent must have been made when his son had the car, but he wants to see if his son will own up to it; he perhaps also wants to shame his son for not having volunteered information about the incident that resulted in the dent.

Other questions may really be expressions of disdain ("You're not seriously thinking of wearing that to dinner, are you?") or requests for undeserved reassurance ("Isn't this fun?"). There are also loaded questions that have no correct answers. (A person yawns at work, and someone asks, "Are we keeping you awake?") At the risk of offending people, you can treat false questions as the remarks they are rather than playing along.

Complex deception: Implicit lies. Some lies are harder to see coming because they are told over time and are crafted of multiple parts. Suppose the parents of a high school student are invested in the idea that their teenage son is an outstanding student. The student may find it is easiest to let his parents believe he is studying at the library every evening when in truth he is out with his friends. He may conspicuously bring home library books, pretend to fret over upcoming tests, and talk earnestly about Shakespeare or chemical reactions. Each piece of his overall deception is small, but each part is a component of a larger falsehood.

Implicit lies do not necessarily contain actual misrepresentations; one can create false impressions without telling an outright lie. "I'm a serious student" or even "I'm going to the library" statements may never be made. Instead, evidence pointing to those conclusions is strategically parceled out. By distributing clues, it is possible to fabricate positive or negative appearances for ourselves or other people. Political campaign managers are experts at this; they may have their candidate pose for photographs with someone associated with a popular cause, even if the candidate has no involvement or interest in that cause.

If a criminal defense lawyer has any choice, he will want a jury to know about his client's volunteer work in the community, distinguished position in his church, and medals he was awarded during military service, all to take the focus away from the possibility that his client committed a crime. Conversely, the prosecutor's job would be made much easier if she could present instances of the defendant's bad behavior all the way back to the third grade when he set his brother's prized plastic model car on fire. The prosecutor wants to paint him as a bad guy, even though he might be charged with burglary, not arson.

People who create appearances of truth by implication may approach others as friends or even admirers. They assemble positive or negative facts to create whatever one-sided picture serves their goals, and their unbalanced emphasis leads others to false conclusions. The technique may be used by advertisers, supervisors, spouses, politicians, corporate management, drug companies, the media, health-care providers, and even religious leaders. Presenting a distorted picture by revealing only positive facts or traits is what people are absolutely expected to do in a sales presentation, at a job interview, and on a first date.

The implicit lie may be constructed to focus on another person's strengths and skills in order to flatter and persuade him. Men who want only sex from a relationship will say and do all sorts of nice things to get a woman's attention without revealing their limited agenda. Their flattery may be sincere, and they may be genuinely charming, but a direct expression of what they are after would not be welcome in most situations, so they pretend to want something more romantic. If a woman asks outright, "Are you just trying to get me into bed?" the man will say no and continue implying that he wants more than sex. Through expressions of curiosity about a woman, generosity, and compliments, a man can build a convincing picture of interest that does not exist. Whether or not he gets what he wants, his presentation eventually proves to be illusory.

Conversely, a person might concentrate on another's flaws to make that person feel worthless and thus more inclined to accept a deal or circumstance than look for another opportunity.

Egotists use implicit lies. They cannot be honest about their goals either, because propping up a simultaneously overinflated and fragile ego is not admirable. The egotist cannot exclaim, "I need you to say nice things about me so I can feel better about myself." If he is not hearing enough good things, he will use tricks that manufacture apparent proof for the self-image he wants. For example, a person who needs to believe he is the only competent person in a situation and is surrounded by idiots might withhold information from others, or pass out confusing or misleading information. Although the other people may then try to behave competently, they can only follow the bad script they have been handed and end up looking foolish. For example, a musician in a band might present a new song to his bandmates with a lead sheet so sketchy and confusing that the others are forced to ask fundamental questions that a competent musician would normally not need to ask. The composer then feels he has permission to answer his fellow musicians' questions in a disdainful tone.

A cruder method is for the egotist to say nice things about herself and coerce others to express agreement. The coercion may be exerted by virtue of holding a position of authority, ridiculing dissenters, or even threatening physical violence.

Because their motivations are often shameful, implicit liars will be quick to assure you of their sincerity, to point out why they are correct about whatever they choose to comment on, or to insist they are only trying to help. Good acting skills provide cover for false flattery and mask the critical intent of negative statements.

People who do not normally create distortions with implicit lies can find the behavior especially disorienting and disturbing. These interactions are set up only to give the implicit liar some benefit. The goal may not be to make anyone feel bad, but that is a frequent effect. The implicit liar's focus is on creating the appearance of a certain reality. An implicit liar may not always be conscious of his methods; he may well be unaware of the destructive effect the behavior has on others.

There is a way to deal with implicit liars. Because the implicit liar is trying to hide his true motivations, you can question his intent. "Are you trying to confuse me?" and "Are you trying to make me feel bad?" are legitimate questions. When challenged, he is never going to admit he is out to create false impressions, but he will stop assuming you can be fooled as easily as he would like. He may even give up.

Implicit liars are best recognized early and then avoided, although spotting them quickly can be difficult. They may be practiced at hiding the overall lie of their agenda, and you may have reasons to want to believe what they say. The people who lie to you in a complimentary fashion can be just as harmful as people who do not seem so nice. Except for someone telling actual white lies, any kind of liar is putting his needs ahead of yours. If you fail to see the deceit, you may find yourself working on a project with one, dating one, or even married to one.

Even more challenging than spotting the manipulative individual is seeing the implicit lies of a corporation, a political candidate, or a public personality with whom you have no direct interaction. Yet it is still the same matter of recognizing the selective truths, deliberate omissions, and underlying agenda. While you will never be able to call the bluff of all of the implicit liars in the world, you can recognize their tactics and expose them or at least refuse to draw the conclusions they want.

Seeing the Type of Lie Means Seeing the Lie

As with most human behavior, lying follows recognizable patterns. The form of a lie may be more evident than the substance of a lie. By keeping in mind the most common ways lies are told, you are much more likely to realize a lie is being presented in the moment. That may be your best opportunity to do something about it, whether that means letting the liar know he or she has not fooled you or immediately rejecting the conclusion you are being asked to draw.

3

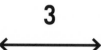

Lessons from Law: Methods for Seeing Truth

his chapter presents detailed explanations of processes used in jury trials. You can adapt some of the rules used by trial courts to help you get to the truth in your own life, since a central function of civil and criminal courts is to determine the truth about what has happened in a given situation.

Judges and juries are called upon to interpret the presentations of lawyers and make significant decisions. There is inherent drama in trials; by the time a case goes before a jury, the dispute is sharply defined. It is not surprising that for decades the process of finding the truth in a legal setting has been the background of novels and television shows. Perhaps the purest form was the *Perry Mason* television series in which Mason, a criminal defense attorney, was routinely able to elicit confessions from witnesses during his cross-examinations at trial.[1] When witnesses broke down on the stand, viewers were able to share in Mason's triumph, which was the culmination of his cleverness and determination and his team's excellent investigative work. Within an hour, the show presented a puzzle, solved it, and demonstrated that justice could be served.

Other courtroom and police dramas followed, as well as crime-scene investigation shows, all playing off the idea that the truth is out there somewhere, and if we are clever enough, we can find it. Although these shows have varied in format and level of sophistication, their protagonists have shared the common trait of an obsessive desire to find the truth. Audiences find these people admirable because of that characteristic; we all have curiosity about the world and a desire to determine what is real. It is reassuring to think the truth *is* out there, and all we need to do is hunt it down. Much like the protagonists in TV shows, we encounter unknowns in daily life. Parents must figure out whether their kids are telling them the truth; investors must decide whom to trust with their money; people seeking a relationship must decide whom to date. Just as a jury weighs the evidence presented, we must also weigh evidence, become convinced of facts, and make decisions based on what we come to believe.

In a trial, each side does its best to put a spin on the evidence; the overall goal is to win, which may or may not involve revealing the truth. Witnesses who are otherwise forthright and honest may not hesitate to bend facts when their liberty or financial interests are at stake. As any trial lawyer will tell you, what matters in trial is not what actually happened but what a judge or jury can be made to believe happened.

Our judicial system provides tools to see through spin. While imperfect, modern jurisprudence has evolved over hundreds of years, much of it adopted from English common law. The judicial system embodies collective wisdom about how humans go about making decisions. Judges become experts at spotting the slightest hint of deception from a lawyer or litigant. The rules used in trials are designed to help jurors reach the same level of sophistication that good judges develop.

Looking at the broader picture for a moment, the motivation of the litigants is also worth bearing in mind. Emotions often play a role in whether a case ever goes to trial. There are lawsuits that are overtly about emotional distress, but more frequently the powerful desire to be vindicated gives an injured party the additional motivation needed to tolerate the stress of litigation. For example, patients are more likely to sue a doctor who has not only made a mistake but who then compounds it by appearing arrogant or uncaring. After University of Michigan Health System hospitals urged their doctors to apologize for mistakes up front, malpractice suits and notices of intent to sue were cut roughly by half. Michael Woods, a physician and co-author of *Healing Words: The Power of Apology in Medicine*, observes that a patient may be bothered by her doctor's attitude more than by the doctor's medical error.[2] Patients may see a trial as a vehicle to win back their dignity and hold accountable a doctor who has harmed them physically or emotionally.

What are the specific trial procedures that can be applied to our own lives? Although state and federal systems have different rules for trials, the principles are essentially the same. Let us look at a hypothetical case to illustrate the steps.

At around 5:00 a.m., while the sky was still dark, a bakery delivery truck lost one of its wheels on the freeway. The truck came to rest in the fast lane, just over the crest of a small hill. The driver placed two flares behind the truck, and the first few vehicles that approached were able to avoid the truck. The next car was not, and a chain reaction collision ensued in which several drivers were injured. The motorists brought lawsuits against the bakery, as well as each other.

Pretrial Discovery: Fact Gathering

Suppose I am representing the bakery that owns the truck and employs its driver. My first step is to gather the information that allows me to analyze the potential liability of my client and prepare the case for trial. I may subpoena documents, send written questions (interrogatories) to the other side, and obtain oral testimony under oath that is preserved for trial in written transcripts (depositions). I would obtain the police report, which will include some law enforcement analysis about the cause of the accident. The bakery may have its own internal report about what happened.

I would locate the driver and discuss what happened the morning of the accident. He might tell me things that he did not want to put in the company's written report, and I could ask questions nobody else has asked him. Perhaps he tells me that per company policy, the truck was supposed to carry five flares, but he could only find two. Or perhaps he tells me there were five flares, but he was so rattled he forgot to use them all. Whatever I can find out is important to know immediately; I do not want any surprises during the trial.

Then I might examine the maintenance history of the truck and discover that a new tire had been mounted on the truck a few days before the accident. On the theory that the tire store did not adequately tighten the wheel, I might bring the tire store into the lawsuit.

By this time, the other drivers involved in the accident may have responded to my written questions; their oral depositions would be scheduled. Because answers to the written questions were most likely crafted mainly by the drivers' lawyers, the responses will contain as little factual information as possible, under the theory that any information submitted can and will be used against the person making the representation. In an oral deposition, however, people have to be more spontaneous when asked questions. Cagey deponents will still use tricks to try to avoid giving meaningful answers ("I don't remember *exactly. . . .*"), or they may provide information that has only a peripheral relationship to the topic and is not truly responsive. Or they may try to get away with general answers:

Q: How fast were you going?

A: I was going with the flow of traffic.

Q: Were your headlights on?

A: I would have had them on that time of the morning.

Q: What are your injuries?

A: I hurt all over.

I would not be doing my job if I let someone get away with these vague responses. Rather than accepting the "flow of traffic" answer, I would ask if that meant faster or slower than sixty miles per hour and continue to narrow it down until we arrived at the most exact estimate the witness was willing to give. I would ask for a specific recollection about whether the headlights were on. I would ask about the driver's injuries in detail, naming every part of the body and asking detailed questions about the symptoms the driver was experiencing in each one.

Typically, lawyers coach their clients to say as little as possible and to volunteer nothing in a deposition. It is remarkable how little a witness may say in response to a question, while still being technically responsive:

Q: Do you recall the first thing you saw as you crested the hill that morning?

A: Yes.

A taciturn witness forces the questioning attorney to ask very precise questions, which may make it more difficult to get a comprehensive picture. Of course, it is crucial to obtain all the facts, because a driver in this situation may eventually be compelled to admit that just before the accident she was speeding, did not have her lights on, was talking on a cell phone, or was retrieving a burning cigarette from the floor of her car.

Well-planned, relentless questioning is critical, yet one of the most effective techniques is when the attorney successfully engages the witness in a real conversation. The more casual the tone of the deposition, the less guarded and more revealing the witness may be.

After gathering the preliminary facts with these tools, I can determine if settlement before trial is a sensible option. If it is obvious my client is at fault, I may not recommend going to trial. If, conversely, it becomes obvious my client is not at fault, I will recommend a trial rather than paying an unjustified settlement. There may also be some middle ground, where uncertain facts lead to a compromise settlement.

→ Start by getting the facts; competent investigation takes time and careful planning.

Extraneous Information

Before a trial begins, the attorneys may ask the judge to rule on the admission or exclusion of specific evidence. The court is routinely asked to prohibit any mention of whether the defendant is covered by insurance. The theory is that the jury must determine the facts free of any concerns about where the money is coming from; the question of insurance would be too much of a distraction. The motion regarding insurance is routinely granted, meaning that it is assumed juries would not be able to put the issue of insurance coverage out of their minds. In other words, jurors are presumed to be unable to ignore certain things they know. Jurors' ignorance of certain information is carefully guarded so that they can focus completely on the pertinent questions.

In 2004, a jury in Alameda County, California, sentenced Stuart Alexander to death for killing three meat inspectors at his plant.[3] A video of the killings caught on security cameras was played for the jury. Alexander's defense attorney, Michael Ogul, said that he believed the jurors sentenced Alexander to death rather than to life in prison because they watched the killings for themselves on the video rather than hearing about the murders from witnesses. The prosecutor turned an objective truth into an even more powerful subjective truth. For Stuart Alexander, this was more than a philosophical distinction, because the shift to subjective truth meant the death penalty.[4]

In the hypothetical bakery-truck case, if there had been gory photographs of any of the injured drivers or their passengers, the attorneys for those people would want the jury to see the photos. In representing the bakery, I would want to keep the photos away from the jurors. Although the nature of the injuries would be presented through the testimony of treating physicians, bloody photographs would have a more extreme effect than clinical descriptions. Jurors are more likely to award damages, and to award higher damages, if they view depictions of injuries. In reality, a superficial wound might bleed massively, while a seriously disabling injury might not bleed at all. Since we base decisions largely on visceral reactions, gory photographs could skew the results.

It is worth emphasizing that most of us cannot sort out objective facts from facts tinged with emotion. We all like to think we know better. But that is exactly the problem; when we *believe* we can make objective judgments in situations in which we are emotionally involved, we are kidding ourselves.

Using our emotions as a guide for some decisions is perfectly appropriate. Sometimes we have a bad feeling about a person or situation and stay away, as we should. But our emotions can make us less able to perceive objective truth. We can all make the mistake of responding to the wrong cues.

→ Be skeptical of any presentation to which you have an emotional reaction, because you may be responding to a carefully planted sideshow, not the main event.
→ Actively look for elements in any presentation that are not actually pertinent but are included only to manipulate your feelings.

I Am Not Prejudiced! Jury Selection

Although most trials require only twelve jurors, many more people are called upon to appear for potential duty at the start of the proceeding. The judge may quickly dismiss those who have an obvious bias and will not be able to decide the matter fairly. Someone who had been shot during a bank holdup would certainly be excused from serving on a jury for a trial in which the defendant was being charged with armed bank robbery. The attorneys also have a limited number of discretionary challenges, allowing them to excuse jurors they believe might be prejudiced against their client for more subtle reasons.

Potential jurors come to the courthouse with a lifetime of preconceived ideas that guide their decisions. When asked, most will sincerely claim they *could* put any prejudices aside but that they do not actually *have* any prejudices. In reality, all of us have some beliefs that amount to prejudices, whether or not we label them that way. Once we start applying a preconceived idea, few among us will spend much time reflecting on it, and even the person who is aware it may be a prejudice may believe it would be a mistake to admit that publicly.

Before you think, "But I don't have any prejudices!" consider that we all construct our picture of reality from many sources. Not all of those sources are accurate, and sometimes we misunderstand them. Prejudices can grow out of incorrect information, misinterpretation, limited information, or fear. Because of a few experiences, we may start generalizing about racial or gender groups or other categories of people. For instance, the owner of a small business who has struggled with problematic employees for years may be inherently unsympathetic to someone's bringing a legal claim against an employer. The business owner has come to view employees more as troublemakers than as human beings deserving empathy. She probably does not see this as a prejudice but rather as the way things are in the world. A person dissatisfied with his own past medical care may be far more likely than the average juror to find a doctor at fault in a medical malpractice case. He does not see himself as biased but as well informed.

We apply these types of ideas to the world automatically. Second-guessing our beliefs slows us down, and confidence is more pleasant than uncertainty. At the same time, the preconceived ideas we will not reconsider can interfere with our ability to take in new information. In high-stakes trials, attorneys employ jury consultants to help them spot jurors' prejudices. In any trial, the attorneys themselves try to determine how each juror is likely to view the litigants' positions. Attorneys are usually allowed to ask at least a few questions of each prospective juror. Although every lawyer approaches choosing a jury a little differently, a lawyer is mainly interested in:

Jurors who have personal experience with the subject matter. In the case of the disabled bakery truck, a potential juror who had been injured in a freeway accident would probably be rejected by counsel for the bakery. That potential juror might be too quick to assume his own experiences were similar to those of an injured party in the lawsuit, or he might feel he had never been fully compensated and view the trial as a chance to see justice done—even if the circumstances are only superficially similar.

Jurors who assume authority. Some jurors see themselves as having more power than anyone else in the courtroom, and these jurors exercise considerable freedom in making factual determinations. Others look intently for cues from the judge and try especially hard to follow the law exactly as it is explained to them. These factors influence their decision making.

Jurors who believe we must all play the cards we are dealt. Those who believe in rugged individualism and the idea that everyone in the United States has an equal opportunity to be successful may not be sympathetic to criminal defendants or accident victims. They may view all bad acts as deserving of punishment and see pain and suffering from an injury as a fact of life that people should tough out.

Jurors who are guided primarily by emotion or primarily by rationality. People who base their decisions largely on emotions may proceed with confidence because they are deeply aware of how they feel. In fact, they may be acting impulsively based on incomplete or emotionally tinged information. People who make decisions by following a rational, fact-gathering process may not be influenced by graphic presentations and may be less amenable to considering extenuating circumstances. A juror's degree of emotionality or rationality will end up favoring one side or the other.

Jurors with an axe to grind. Some jurors may want to serve because they have strong personal beliefs about issues involved in the case or about issues they *think* are involved in the case. If they want to champion one side, they are unlikely to see or hear evidence that conflicts with their agenda.

Jurors' age, gender, ethnic identification, income level, and cultural background. People tend to understand and sympathize most with those they perceive as similar to themselves.

You can learn from the jury selection process by asking yourself what type of juror you might be in a particular setting. Are your past experiences getting in the way of seeing the present? Do you want to see things a certain way so badly that you are not seeing them accurately? If you are an emotional person, you can assume you do not have all the facts and practice focusing on them. If you are a rational person, allowing your feelings to be a factor in your assessments may give you a new perspective.

→ In any situation in which you must make important decisions, consider how the truth may be obscured by:

- your personal experiences
- your attitudes about authority
- your beliefs about how much people can change their lives
- your use of emotions and rationality
- your personal agenda(s)
- your tendency to identify with people like yourself

Good Questions Get Good Answers: Statement of the Case

Once a jury is seated, the judge may read a neutral statement about the events in question. In the bakery truck case, the jurors would be told the basic facts of the accident and advised that after the presentation of the evidence, they will be called upon to decide who was at fault and the amount of compensation an injured party is entitled to, if any. As you can imagine, the judge's neutral statement will not contain characterizations such as "victim of a horrific accident" or "unfairly maligned defendant."

In our own lives, if we do not carefully frame our questions, the truth about a topic may never emerge. Unlike the jurors in a trial, who must sit back and listen to presentations designed by lawyers, we have the luxury of designing the questions to be answered.

→ For example, if you are dating with marriage in mind, you can frame questions to find out:

- Does this person want to have children?
- What are his/her financial ambitions?
- Does she/he value what I consider most important in life?
- Does she/he like to have fun in the same way I do?

Less significant issues can be left to intuition and good chemistry, but it is clearly helpful to keep in mind what the overall goal is and what the most crucial questions are.

→ The sooner you define the important questions, the sooner you will obtain meaningful answers.

People Who Tell You What to Think: Opening Statements

Once the judge has read the statement of the case to the jury, the attorneys are allowed to speak directly to the group and announce what they expect to prove through the evidence presented in the trial. Jurors tend to make up their minds by the end of the opening statements. This is not surprising, given that each attorney will tell the best story she can, knowing that the opposing attorney is sure to remind the jury about any exaggerations or fabrications when closing statements are made. Yet it is critical that jurors not fall asleep after hearing opening statements, because attorneys can and do sometimes overstate their cases.

A witness may also not say what is expected, or evidence may just not have the desired effect.

→ Engaging summaries have the power to influence, but in our own lives it is unwise to accept other people's characterizations about important matters. Seek out proof; do not rely on others' presentations.

We Are Constantly Being Offered Unreliable Evidence: Hearsay

The hearsay rule prohibits witnesses from repeating the statements of others. There are exceptions, such as when a declarant believes he or she is near death. It is presumed that a person about to die wishes to clear his or her conscience and also sees nothing to lose by telling the truth. Although the person who made the original statement cannot be cross-examined, the witness's fear of imminent death gives the repetition of the statement high credibility value. But normally, second-hand statements are inherently unreliable. We have no idea what the original speaker's motivations might have been at the time the statement was made; we cannot be sure the witness is repeating the statement accurately; we do not get to hear the original speaker's tone of voice; and there is no opportunity to ask the original speaker any clarifying questions.

In daily life, we constantly hear, "Then she said to me . . . ," and we are expected to believe whatever follows. Yet these repeated statements may be embellished to make them more colorful, or they may be remembered incorrectly. They might be nothing but rumor or gossip that never had any basis in fact. Statements repeated by a third party deserve the same skepticism in our lives as in court. They can be especially insidious when we know the people involved and are able to imagine the original speaker uttering the words. However, imagination is no substitute for accuracy.

→ Treat second-hand statements with caution.

Presentation of the Plaintiff's Evidence: Persuasion at Work

Depending on the type of trial, different standards of proof are required. In most civil cases, the plaintiff's burden is only to present a preponderance of the evidence. If there is slightly more evidence in the plaintiff's favor, the plaintiff wins. If the plaintiff's evidence leaves the jury unsure of which side to believe, the defendant wins. Some situations call for the complaining party to prove his or her case by stronger "clear and convincing" evidence. In a criminal case, the prosecutor must meet an even higher standard by showing that the defendant is guilty "beyond a reasonable doubt."

In the example bakery truck case, the injured driver of the first car to hit the truck would endeavor to prove his case by describing for the jury his experience on the day of the accident. He would wish to establish that he was traveling at a reasonable speed, was attentive, and encountered the disabled truck with no opportunity to avoid it. He would want to establish that any safety measures taken by the truck driver after the breakdown were inadequate—that reflectors or flares placed behind the truck were too few in number and/or were placed too close to the truck to afford any benefit to drivers traveling at freeway speeds. This plaintiff would also need to establish that he suffered damages from this accident—that his injuries were real and that they resulted in medical bills, time lost from work, and pain and suffering.

The defense is entitled to cross-examine witnesses and attempt to raise doubts about their veracity, point out any contradictions with their earlier deposition testimonies, and bring out details their own attorneys never asked about. The plaintiff's attorney may call other witnesses, such as the other drivers, the doctors who treated the plaintiff, engineers who analyzed the accident, and police officer(s) who responded and wrote reports.

The evidence must be factual; except for the opinions of expert witnesses with special expertise, lay witness opinions are allowed on very limited topics. Courtroom testimony is unlike everyday conversation, which may include a mix of the speaker's opinions, subjective impressions, speculations, and facts. The language of testimony also tends to be more precise than ordinary conversation, in which we speak in incomplete sentences and routinely interrupt one other.

As a whole, the presentation of the plaintiff's case must be skillful and persuasive. Jurors resent clumsy, obvious attempts to manipulate their opinions. The best plaintiffs appear sincere and somewhat stoic, downplaying rather than exaggerating their complaints.

→ Jurors are generally not allowed to ask any questions during the presentation of evidence throughout a trial, and they are expressly prohibited from undertaking their own research. Unlike a juror, when you are facing a decision, if the quantity or quality of available facts is not satisfactory, you can seek out more information. Take advantage of the opportunity.

Presentation of the Defendant's Evidence: The Accused

In theory, a defendant does not have to put on a defense at all, because the plaintiff must do the work of convincing the jury that his or her version of the truth is the correct one. But in the case of the disabled truck, the bakery might try to show that the driver who became injured was approaching too fast, was inattentive, and/or did not really suffer the injuries being claimed. The defendant will wish to create so much doubt that the plaintiff will have difficulty proving anything.

Both plaintiffs and defendants may lie by omission. The phrase "the truth, the whole truth, and nothing but the truth" attempts to address that problem. The driver who claims he was not speeding but neglects to mention that he did not see the bakery truck because he was busy sending a text message is hardly telling the whole truth.

Even eyewitnesses can make mistakes. On April 23, 2007, Jerry Miller became the 200th person in the United States to be cleared by DNA evidence. He had served twenty-four years for rape because of faulty witness testimony; technology to prove his innocence was not available at the time of his conviction. The evidence from the old case eventually implicated another man, whose DNA profile was in an FBI database.[5]

A 2004 University of New South Wales study, reported in the *Journal of Experimental Social Psychology*, concluded that people who were in a bad mood gave more accurate versions of what they observed, while people in good moods were not as observant.[6] A 1989 survey by researchers Kassin, Ellsworth, and Smith concluded that jurors tend to rely too heavily on the apparent confidence of witnesses.[7]

→ Be aware that even what appears certain may not be accurate.

Closing Statements: More Argument

In closing statements, the attorneys are again allowed to address the jury directly. Although everyone in the courtroom has seen and heard the exact same evidence, it is now a matter of deciding how that evidence should be interpreted. The attorneys put a positive spin on the evidence their witnesses have provided, and they criticize the credibility and/or importance of testimony from the other side. Moreover, they argue that all the evidence leads to an inevitable result in favor of their client.

If all the available evidence did indeed lead to an automatic conclusion, the case probably would have been settled out of court by this point. But whether flares or reflectors were far enough behind the disabled bakery truck, whether Mr. A's back really still hurts, and whether Mrs. B's knee problem is actually the same problem she has had for ten years, may all be open to debate.

I once heard an interesting closing argument presented by a criminal prosecutor that involved the use of an old percolator-style coffee pot. He held up its center rod, remarking that the defense attorney would have the jury believe it was a telescope. He held up the perforated top of the grounds container, adding that the defense attorney would have the jury believe that this was the cover for a shower drain. Displaying the metal basket, he said it could also be called a colander. But then he assembled the pieces, and he did not need to say that the pieces actually formed a coffee pot.

The lawyer for Jeff Skilling, the former president of Enron who in 2006 was sentenced to twenty-four years in prison for fraud, ridiculed testimony about secret agreements at Enron called "bear hugs." He said they were in a trial, not a petting zoo.[8] His comment made people in the courtroom laugh. Of course, whatever any secret agreements were called by the people at Enron had nothing to do with whether they existed, and nothing to do with whether they were illegal. But if a concept can be made to sound silly, it loses its importance. If the secret agreements had been called something more sinister, such as "snake bites," it would have been more difficult to laugh it off.

→ Labels do matter. If a characterization is entertaining, it colors our perceptions. The next time you buy a product, consider how its labeling affects your sense of its worth.

Jury Instructions and Admonitions

At the conclusion of a jury trial, the judge reads a set of instructions to the jury about its duties. One instruction admonishes the jury not to be swayed by bias, prejudice, or sympathy. My own trial experience has convinced me that while jurors want to do the right thing, their idea of the right thing is the product of their life experiences, including the biases, prejudices, and sympathies they have inherited and assembled over the years. A juror may not believe she has any biases, prejudices, or sympathies to disregard.

The jury is told not to decide anything by the flip of a coin, not to speculate about excluded evidence, not to engage in experiments, and not to visit the scene where the events occurred, but to decide the case based *only* on the evidence presented during the trial.

→ Use only meaningful evidence in your own decision making. Using speculation or chance is not decision making at all.

Deliberations

The jury is regarded as a group of equals who should express their views to one another openly and bring a variety of interpretations to the same facts. They are charged with the task of determining who is telling the truth and what the final outcome should be. In a California civil trial, a consensus decision means that nine out of twelve jurors agree on the outcome. Deliberations may take less than an hour or go on for days. A foreperson is elected to keep the discussions on track, but otherwise the only distinction among jurors is the force of their personalities.

The presentation and consideration of evidence in a trial is never as neat and clean as the *Perry Mason* series would have had us believe. Witnesses may be nervous, inarticulate, or unavailable to testify. Their recollections may be poor. They rarely break down and admit to lying while under cross-examination on the witness stand. The attorneys may not give clear presentations. The trial may be repeatedly interrupted by evidentiary objections, whispered meetings between the lawyers and the judge, or by witness-scheduling problems. Regardless, jurors must decide what the puzzle pieces they have been handed represent, even if some of the key pieces seem to be missing completely.

Discussions resembling jury deliberations may occur in the work-place or within families. Sometimes the purpose is not to discover the truth or the best idea, but to create the appearance of a cooperative process, while reinforcing the authority of whoever is actually in charge. In a workplace meeting, for example, after employees are invited to submit their ideas, they may be told why their ideas will not work, or their suggestions may simply be ignored. At other times, communications are genuine, with successful leaders soliciting and using input from the people in the trenches.

Most of our deliberations are actually with ourselves. Because our internal deliberations are not set up with the formality of jury deliberations or business meetings, we may ponder things when we have time and when we are in the mood. Nobody shuts us into a deliberation room and makes us think about the issues in our lives. We may contemplate a single problem in separate sessions while driving a car, while gardening, and then again in the shower. This allows us to consider issues from different moods and perspectives, although without the benefit of structure or input from others.

→ Solicit the opinions of others in your decision-making process; they may have valuable perspectives and are usually flattered to be asked.

→ Give structure to the important considerations in your life. Decide what information you need, gather it, and find a quiet place where you can sit and think. Your decisions are worthy of formal contemplation.

4

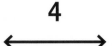

Thirty-Six Places Where the Truth Hides

Ask anyone if he wants the truth, and he will probably say yes. Ask if he always gets the truth, and he will probably say no. As mentioned earlier, assembling the truth is like putting together a puzzle, except we do not always know if we have all the pieces. People may be hiding pieces from us; sometimes we have them and just do not know where they fit.

There are numerous reasons the truth eludes us. This chapter describes thirty-six places where the truth may be hidden.

Expectation and Desire

In May 1941, the formidable new German battleship *Bismarck* was menacing shipping in the North Atlantic. The fully modern *Bismarck* was equipped with aircraft tracking equipment calibrated to defend against the faster modern planes the Germans expected would be attacking. Soon after being launched, *Bismarck* destroyed one of Britain's most respected military ships, the *Hood*. The British became determined to sink the *Bismarck*, but only outdated biplanes, all Fairey Swordfishes, were available for an aerial assault.[1] These flew at less than 100 miles per hour, had canvas skins, and carried a single torpedo each. There has been speculation that the slow speed of the Swordfish and their low flight altitude gave them an advantage over ships expecting faster airplanes flying higher, and that, in addition, the thin canvas skins of these biplanes did not provide enough resistance to trigger the detonation of the modern shells fired at them. One of the Swordfish was able to score a hit that disabled the *Bismarck*'s rudder, rendering the huge ship unable to maneuver and allowing the British navy to sink it. For all the *Bismarck*'s size and new equipment, its designers had failed to appreciate that extraordinarily slow and flimsy aircraft might be its undoing.

Just as seeing what we expect to see can blind us to the truth, seeing what we want to see can blind us as well. For years, home equity lenders stressed how much immediate cash they could put into a borrower's hands; they did not emphasize escalating interest rates, how long the loan would put off the day when the homeowner owned the house free and clear, or how becoming overextended would jeopardize home ownership itself. People borrowed equity because they wanted to believe easy money was available. Sometimes people believe what they would like to be true.

→ Be aware that impressions come most easily when we expect or want them; the truth is less evident when it is not anticipated or desired.

Distraction

Distraction is one of the most common tactics of persuaders. When questioned on weak points, they steer the topic of conversation to something else. Yet anyone who wants to make a good decision needs the truth, not distractions.

It is not just others who distract us from truths; we can do the same thing to ourselves. While we claim we want the truth, we have to be able to handle it even when it is uncomfortable. Life offers many potential distractions from truths. Distractions may range from addiction to drugs, alcohol, gambling, sex, or computer games, to hobbies, television, the Internet, and innumerable other pastimes, some harmless and some harmful. If you are habitually preoccupied, you cannot spend as much time putting pieces of the truth together. Like the difference between traveling alone in a foreign country and traveling with a group, you will not be as engaged with your surroundings when there are more familiar interactions to turn to.

→ Be aware of what distracts you from recognizing what is real.

Seductive Interpretations

Objective facts are mixed, often unrecognizably, with our subjective impressions of the world. Sometimes we interpret things in a way that makes them more palatable. Advertisers, campaign managers, and spin masters tap into our desire to construe facts in particular ways. They supply plausible, even if completely unsubstantiated, reasons for us to believe what we want to believe. The most blatant of all may be the message from the advertiser to the consumer: "You deserve this." How would the advertiser know? But we may be willing to skip over gaps in logic when we want something; sometimes all it takes is a little encouragement.

Labeling

Labels provide a quick way to spin undesirable facts. It is easier to give problems names than to examine them closely, let alone find solutions. Labels can help us feel better while steering us away from the truth. Giving an employee an important-sounding job title instead of a raise costs nothing, but it may have the same effect of satisfying the employee. We are surrounded by euphemistic labels: the "Peacekeeper" was the name of a missile. The "Healthy Forests Initiative" was criticized by the Sierra Club as a stealth measure to benefit logging companies.[2] "Collateral damage" means killing innocent bystanders, "preowned" means used, while "corporate downsizing" means people are getting fired.

Real estate agents have invented their own labels:

- "cozy" = tiny
- "room to expand" = unbelievably tiny
- "needs TLC" = neglected
- "near transportation" = the freeway noise is horrendous
- "rustic" = rotted
- "classic" = old
- "cute" = cramped
- "lots of character" = possible termite problem

→ Labels are red flags. Use them to recognize when someone is attempting to sell a characterization, not what is underneath it.

Jargon

People in every discipline use some specialized terms to convey the particular concepts they are dealing with. When they forget they are talking to people who do not know their terminology, or when they use it to make themselves sound important, the only truths they convey are about their own ignorance or arrogance.

Stereotyping

Albert McGee, a member of the Chicago Vice Lords gang, which dates back to the 1950s, was interviewed after being incarcerated in the Mississippi State Penitentiary for homicide and drug possession. He said that when he was in trouble, the best thing to do was to tell the police a gang member was threatening his life, and they would "go for it."[3] In other words, even the police, who ought to know better, would believe any negative thing they were told about gang members. As much as we may want to be free of stereotypes and prejudices, we all have some preconceived images that adversely influence our thinking and decision making.

→ There are many situations where it is worthwhile to ask yourself how your preconceived notions are influencing your thought processes.

Resisting Truths We Wish Were False

Events sometimes happen to us for odd reasons with no apparent connection to how we have lived our lives up until that moment. Shallow, stupid people are born into money. Incurable diseases strike good and kind people, while mean, nasty people live long and healthy lives. None of these events seems fair, but they were not caused by a moral system. Our concept of fairness goes back to childhood and is easy to apply. When something goes against how we think the world ought to work, we may resist recognizing that we have to find a way to live with it.

→ Avoid the temptation to conclude, "This isn't fair—I shouldn't have to deal with it." Recognize the reality so you can begin to address the problem.

The Need for a Clear, Comprehensible Answer

When something monumental occurs, especially something sudden such as the assassination of JFK or the 9/11 terrorist attacks, people naturally want to know why it happened. The JFK assassination appeared too significant to be the work of a lone gunman. It seemed logical that a plot approximating the complexity of the presidency itself must have been involved. Or, wanting a more concrete explanation for 9/11, some people invented conspiracy theories implicating the United States government in the attack. Sometimes the truth is less logical or accessible than we would like, so we invent explanations that fit in with how we think things work.

→ Remember, no answer is better than a false answer.

Needing to Be Right

Extreme positions or beliefs can offer the attraction of absolute certainty. But truth is seldom black or white; it is often found in the muddy middle. Any type of zealotry or adherence to dogmatic views of the world leads adherents to disregard anything not already in their belief systems. The truth may be the first casualty in the hunger to be right.

Taking It Personally

If our beliefs are discredited, it can feel as though we ourselves have been discredited. To avoid discarding what feels like a part of ourselves, we may hold onto beliefs that are no longer valid. Pride can get in the way of admitting conceptual mistakes.

My Desires Are All That Matter

A man who loves to hunt is not going to be persuaded to give up his guns by statistics that show the dangers of gun ownership. It does not matter to him that between 1999 and 2005, more than 5,300 people in the United States died from unintentional shootings; or that from 1990 to 2005, two-thirds of domestic homicides involved firearms.[4] Gun-control advocates can bring up the number of children accidentally killed by guns every year, the number of guns stolen and then used to commit crimes, or even the number of gun owners who accidentally shoot their hunting partners. None of these facts matter; the gun owner will argue with the statistics or insist they do not apply to him. What matters to him is that he wants to keep his guns.

On the other side, gun-control advocates will acknowledge few, if any, of the benefits of owning guns. Whenever someone deters a crime with a gun, supporters of gun control dismiss the incident as an exception. They have little response to the problem that criminals would by nature be inclined to keep guns even if guns were outlawed.

Arguments on both sides of an issue can be valid, but to support a position, we usually pay close attention to our own desires and shut the other side out completely.

Adopting Only the Truths That Make Us More Important

Presented with the opportunity to stick out a foot to trip a fleeing, unarmed bank robber on the sidewalk, a person can quickly become a hero. If the bank robber is waving a gun around and there is a chance of getting shot while trying to be a hero, the same person is likely to say, "Not my problem!" While both behaviors make sense under the circumstances, what changes is the thought process. We are more likely to imbue a potential truth with validity when that truth includes an admirable role for us, or is at least unlikely to cause us problems.

Practical Limitations

When events happen one after the other in front of us like dominoes falling, cause and effect are easy to understand. Sometimes all we see is the last domino falling—the moment the bread comes out of the oven, or the day a new car rolls off the assembly line. If we want to understand what led up to that moment, we must either gather more information or make an educated guess. We have limited time and energy; we cannot investigate everything, so we must accept the vast majority of end results without truly understanding everything that went into the process of achieving those results. We can reach false conclusions in the process—for instance, that it is easy to write a hit song or raise good kids, or that being an Olympic gold medal winner is mostly a matter of having natural talent.

Just as we cannot always investigate the past to see what led up to the events of the present, we also miss the billions of events that are occurring simultaneously at any given moment. We remain in one place at a time. Dominoes are falling next door, across the country, and around the world, and we learn about those processes, if at all, not through personal observation but through secondhand information. Our impressions of the past and present are largely made up of ideas, not personal experiences, meaning that we are relying on the truths of others much of the time. Sometimes the truths of others are better than our own observations. They may be more insightful or less filled with distractions, but they may also be abbreviated or crafted to create an appearance that serves a particular goal.

→   Although you necessarily rely on the representations of others, you should always consider the agendas of the people who tell you what you cannot see for yourself.

The Party Line

In a business setting, you may know the truth is contrary to what management says. You may even disagree vehemently. But a successful subordinate, to avoid being seen as a troublemaker, might parrot the company philosophy or party line. After a while, the party line can start to feel familiar, or even faintly true.

The same grudging familiarity can develop in social settings: whether someone's friends include Presbyterians, Libertarians, or gangsters, by associating with them, a person becomes familiar with their ways of thinking. At first, the unfamiliar belief systems of those friends may be a source of friction. But if the association continues, the new beliefs will become familiar, then tolerated, and perhaps finally accepted, if only to make social interactions easier. Over time, foreign beliefs may increasingly seem to make sense and eventually become accepted as truths.

→ Be careful of the temptation to accept what becomes familiar as being true.

Certainty and Simplicity

We prefer certainty and simplicity because they make decisions easier and less anxiety-ridden. Unfortunately, certainty and simplicity are not always good partners. To be sure we have the truth, we need information that may not be readily available. The more information we consider to support a conclusion, the more conflicts or exceptions we are likely to uncover, and thus the more ambiguity we may have to tolerate. Conclusions that arise out of a limited number of facts, or even a single fact, can have tremendous emotional appeal. Politicians sell themselves by presenting oversimplified conclusions. Populations have been persuaded to take part in wars for centuries because the wars were sold as patriotic acts; the messy, horrific details where withheld. Plans less extreme than war, but also simplistically described as solutions, are even easier to sell. Radio talk-show hosts on both sides of the political fence, advertisers, and politicians all serve up easy, uncomplicated conclusions for public consumption. The truth is rarely as simple as their glib assurances would have us believe.

Trampled by Possibilities

Medical students have long been taught, "When you hear hoofbeats, think horses, not zebras." An exotic disease is never the most likely explanation for a set of symptoms. Just as we can oversimplify, we can overcomplicate and overanalyze problems. It may be more interesting to approach problems this way, but considering too many possibilities, particularly bizarre ones, can also cloud the truth.

Limiting Our Inquiries

As we have seen, getting at the truth requires gathering information. Sometimes we have to cast our nets far and wide. In our nets we will find clues to the truth, but we may also find misapprehensions we need to discard. We miss truths we might otherwise discover because of practical limitations on the volume of information we are able to sort through.

Optimism and Pessimism

No one walks into a restaurant expecting to walk out with a case of food poisoning; no one drives to a shoe store expecting to be in an accident on the way. We need to assume that things will work pretty much the same today as they did yesterday. We benefit from not planning for too many pessimistic contingencies, because we would hardly get anything done that way. We do not check the tires every time we pull out of the driveway just in case one of them went flat overnight. Yet if we are too optimistic and do not, for example, spend money on auto insurance, we would be ignoring a potential truth. The world does change a little every day, and to assume nothing can go wrong tomorrow just because nothing went wrong today invites disastrous consequences.

When we fail to recognize that each day is a little different from the previous day, we can also miss the sometimes subtle opportunities those differences present for making our lives better.

→   Keep your eyes open for what has become true just today.

Idealism

The facts do not always exactly match what we want to believe about ourselves, others, human nature, or events. Facts can interfere with the idealized beliefs we want to have—about a spouse, or a movie star or a political representative. We may then wrongly label certain facts as insignificant. It can be more comfortable to pretend certain wrinkles in our belief systems do not exist than to accept that the wrinkles are there.

Aesthetics

Both beauty and ugliness can hide the truth. Frank Lloyd Wright designed stunning pieces of architecture, but his buildings were also known for water-leakage problems.[5] A beautiful face can momentarily overshadow a rotten personality, just as the elegant styling of older Jaguar cars masked their reliability problems. Machinery may have an uninteresting industrial appearance but be rugged and efficient, and people do judge books by their covers.

Believing Someone or Some Thing Is in Charge

"It wasn't meant to be." "Someone must be looking out for me." At times, we can believe the events in our lives are being deliberately coordinated by some outside force. A string of misfortunes can leave us convinced we are being punished, while a run of good luck may suggest we are doing something morally right. It can be tempting to imagine that everything is part of a grand, ultimately sensible plan, even if we do not understand how that plan works.

When we believe in a grand plan, we lose some of our natural curiosity about why things really do happen. Mythical explanations rob us of knowledge and our ability to discover causes and bring about change.

Superficial Evidence

In July 1997, Lee Harding ate some chicken tacos at a Mexican restaurant in Pueblo, Colorado. He thought they tasted "slimy and gross." Harding developed severe stomach cramps, passed bloody stools, and was eventually diagnosed with an *E. coli* infection. Although Harding was sure he had been sickened by the tacos, the Pueblo Health Department insisted on taking samples of the frozen hamburgers remaining from a meal he had also recently eaten with his wife and sister, neither of whom had become ill. A test of the hamburger meat showed the same strain of bacteria that affected Harding and led to a recall of some 35 million pounds of ground beef in August 1997.[6] If Harding's own analysis—based on his opinion of the chicken tacos—had not been questioned, untold numbers of others would have eaten the contaminated beef and become ill. Our own firsthand impressions do not necessarily yield the truth.

Superficial Affinity

In the spring of 1951, Joe DiMaggio saw a newspaper photograph of Marilyn Monroe posing with a baseball player and holding a bat. Imagining himself in the place of that baseball player, DiMaggio arranged to meet Monroe.[7] Their subsequent short-lived marriage needed something more substantial than DiMaggio's fantasy to hold it together. Choices may seem natural because they contain a familiar element, but that element might be far less important than imagined.

What Is In It for Me?

It is natural for everyone to approach situations with some self-interest in mind. But constantly thinking about ourselves gets in the way of seeing the big picture. For example, if you go to a party and you are completely focused on how you look, you might forget that the point of the party is to celebrate your friend's birthday. When we are too focused on ourselves, we miss the broader reality.

Ego

Egotists relentlessly seek proof of their own talents or cleverness, paying much less attention to clues that they may have fallen short. In an obsessive search for evidence of their superiority, they overlook much of the truth about themselves and often much about the accomplishments of others. Few of us are completely free of this tendency to look for reflections of how important we are. We all can be blinded by our egos at times. Sometimes it is worthwhile to put ourselves aside.

The Awful Truth About Ourselves

We do not always want to know what other people really think of us. If we could somehow collect all the negative thoughts others have ever had about us, the effect might be devastating. We do not often ask others—except perhaps those closest to us—"What do you really think of me?" We live much of our lives with only implied answers to that question.

→ Endeavor to learn what others really think of you. If you can keep your ego in check, you may learn a lot through honest feedback.

We are not always comfortable discovering even positive truths about ourselves. For example, positive traits can weigh us down with a greater sense of responsibility.

→ Decide whether you are hiding some of your strengths, and think about whether that is really necessary.
→ Consider whether people you know may be hiding strengths from you and how drawing those out might benefit everyone.

CHAPTER 4

Not Testing Our Limits

Discovering truths about our personal limitations can be a blow to our self-image. It is more fun to imagine we can do things well than to find out we cannot. By never putting ourselves to the test, we can keep ourselves contentedly in the dark. "I could be a great baseball player, screenwriter, chef, entrepreneur, if only . . ."

→ Testing your limits can help you fulfill your true potential.

Believing Virtue Will Be Rewarded

As important as it is to test our limits and discover our strengths, it is also important to recognize that the outside world may not be receptive to our talents at the moment. John Kennedy Toole, the author of the novel *A Confederacy of Dunces*, failed to find a publisher. Years after Mr. Toole's death, through the persistence of his mother and the writer Walker Percy, the manuscript was published and went on to win a Pulitzer Prize.[8] Toole may have believed his manuscript had merit, but the lack of affirmation from others must have made him doubt the value of his work.

It is tempting to think that our good intentions and hard work will be rewarded in the particular way we imagine. We have direct control over our efforts, but not always over how the world receives those efforts. While it would have deprived us of his book, John Kennedy Toole might have been better off going to parties rather than writing fiction. He did not foresee that his hard work would result in crushing disappointment. In reality, anyone's hard work can go unappreciated.

→ Give serious thought to how you spend your time and energy, and whether what you expect in return is realistic.

Ignorance

Immediately after September 11, 2001, the U.S. government began looking for Osama bin Laden, because he was believed to be directly behind the terrorist attacks on the United States. Despite all the intelligence resources and technology at the United States' disposal, bin Laden managed to slip away and remain hidden. He was not found until 2011. Sometimes we just do not have enough information to resolve even critical problems.

But sometimes people feign ignorance when they simply want to avoid answering a direct question. For example, former secretary of defense Donald Rumsfeld engaged in the following exchange at a Department of Defense news briefing in February 2002, a year before the United States invaded Iraq.

> **Reporter**: Could I follow up, Mr. Secretary, on what you just said, please? In regard to Iraq weapons of mass destruction and terrorists, is there any evidence to indicate that Iraq has attempted to or is willing to supply terrorists with weapons of mass destruction? Because there are reports that there is no evidence of a direct link between Baghdad and some of these terrorist organizations.

> **Rumsfeld**: Reports that say that something hasn't happened are always interesting to me, because as we know, there are known knowns; there are things we know we know. We also know there are known unknowns; that is to say we know there are some things we do not know. But there are also unknown unknowns—the ones we don't know we don't know.[9]

→ The safest approach even in familiar situations is to assume your knowledge is incomplete and constantly be on the lookout for additional elements you are not considering.

→ Be aware that others may not be as ignorant as they pretend to be.

Preserving the Mystery

It is irritating when someone reveals the surprise ending of a movie. Because our lives are lived out much like a story, too much information can take away its mystery or spoil a sense of adventure. We may not want to have a roadmap showing what lies ahead, because we want to discover life's surprises as they come along.

Fear of Fantasy

Just as faint sounds are easier to hear when they are amplified, our true desires are easier to recognize when they are amplified through fantasy. If the fantasies seem too grand, too dangerous, or too frivolous, we may dismiss them. As long as we keep the distinction between fantasies and actual possibilities clearly in mind, fantasies are a great tool for recognizing the kernels of truth at their core.

Protecting Others

We routinely shelter children from the truth. If a child observes someone being arrested, sees a homeless person, or asks, "Mommy, what's a hooker?" she may be given an incomplete or false explanation. Elderly people are also sometimes protected from the truth, and children of all ages know better than to tell their parents the truth about everything in their lives. We lie constantly, believing that we are protecting one another's sense of well-being.

Pretending Problems Do Not Exist

As former Vice President Al Gore pointed out in his film about climate change, the truth is not always convenient. The truth can take away the comfortable pretense that there is nothing wrong and thus that nothing needs fixing. Recognizing the truth may mean we have to change our plans, thoughts, or behaviors, whether the issue is global warming or our physical health.

Believing Perfect Choices Exist

Imagining that we are making the right choice (rather than the best choice) oversimplifies reality. By labeling any choice as "right," we give the choice an aura of perfection. In any situation, all we can do is make the best choice among the options available.

The Truth Can Come Unexpectedly

Scottish bacteriologist Alexander Fleming's laboratory was often cluttered. He would leave glass culture dishes sitting out unwashed for a week or so after doing initial studies on a bacterial culture. In September 1928, he noticed that the bacteria surrounding a green mold in one of the unwashed dishes had been dissolved. The mold was penicillin.[10] Had Fleming been more fastidious about keeping a tidy laboratory, he might well have missed one of the most important discoveries in medicine. Fleming did not plan the specific discovery he made, but he knew enough to recognize and then investigate the unexpected.

The Benefits of Illusion

Christopher Reeve, the actor who portrayed Superman and was paralyzed in an accident in 1995, had both the will and the resources to sustain the hope that he would walk again. He formed the Christopher Reeve Foundation, promoted spinal cord research, and surprised his doctors by regaining some minor movements in his extremities before his death in 2004.[11] He never did walk again, but his life may have been greatly improved by his conviction that he might.

The odds of winning the California SuperLotto Plus are one in 41,416,353,[12] although thousands upon thousands of people buy tickets.

For a dollar, the vague dream of becoming a multimillionaire becomes a tangible possibility. The odds of becoming a movie star, rock star, best-selling novelist, or renowned photographer or painter are not a whole lot better, but people still pursue those dreams. Patent examiners completed 332,000 patent applications by hopeful inventors in 2006 alone, the largest number ever.[13] Some vigorously defend the right to hope and dream by pointing to people who did beat the odds: someone who did win the lottery, or Beatle John Lennon, whose aunt lectured him that he would never make a living with his guitar. They will not mention the millions who tore up their losing lottery tickets or the untold thousands of garage bands that never left the garage.

→ Bear in mind that hope is priceless. Objective truth should sometimes take a back seat.

5

⟵──────⟶

Detecting Deception

There are many ways to prevent lies from being told, and there are many ways to detect lies. Varying situations and different types of lies call for different methods of detection.

Prevention

Countless lies are told that serve little purpose, and these are best dealt with before they are ever spoken. Children and adults lie when they anticipate that the truth will not be acceptable. Because that belief is so often formed in secret, it does not benefit from anyone else's perspective or other reality check. If a man lies about his education because he is ashamed that he did not go beyond the eighth grade, he is assuming others will look down on him if he speaks the truth. His assumption may be wrong; it might be that the majority of people would sympathize, or admire what he has been able to accomplish despite his limited education. If he never tells the truth, he will never discover his lie is unnecessary.

Prevention is a simpler and more effective strategy than the tricky business of looking for clues about lying, hunting for evidence that our suspicions are correct, or confronting the liar, then countering his denials. Lying creates suspicion and destroys relationships. To the extent we can convince people it is unnecessary to lie, we can save everyone a lot of trouble.

While it may seem unreasonable to have to go out of our way to help others be honest with us—should they not be honest anyway?—the reality is that people frequently believe lies are necessary. Common reasons people make misrepresentations include:

- desiring financial gain
- disguising motivation (Saying "I don't want to keep you on the phone" instead of "I'd like to hang up now")
- being unwilling to admit ignorance
- wishing to appear likeable
- wanting to pursue or conceal romantic/sexual interest
- needing to flatter a boss
- attempting to cover up mistakes or bad behavior
- wanting to appear important
- intending to harm others through false rumors or gossip
- avoiding association with bad news or failures

Once we recognize a person's motivations and the subjects they are most likely to lie about, we can make their lies less necessary. We will rarely have an opportunity to be as direct as, "I know you have only an eighth-grade education, but I don't hold it against you." But if a man avoids talking about education, or you hear him inappropriately using complex words, you may sense the underlying issue and his embarrassment. You could then remark about someone you admire who had little formal schooling. Your statements are not likely to spark a confession about any past exaggerations, but his misrepresentations will suddenly become less necessary, at least with you. He will trust you more, and he may even be less inclined to lie about other topics. On the other hand, you can be sure that if you do *not* pay any attention to his feelings, he is never going to trust you completely.

Paying attention to children's feelings is even more important. A father who flies into a rage with his kids and tells them they are horrible every time they reveal something he does not like also guarantees they will stop sharing their lives with him. If the children have to guess about what he might not like, they will err on the side of caution. The father will then have a distant, dishonest relationship with his children.

Many siblings, coworkers, and even spouses have constricted relationships in which only limited, safe subjects are discussed. If too much unpleasantness has already ensued, their interactions embody hundreds of lies by omission, and then sometimes deliberate lies are added to mask those omissions.

Conversely, understanding and empathy promote honesty. This is not a suggestion that we can or should communicate loving acceptance whenever someone tells us something that makes us justifiably angry. It would be dishonest to hide our reactions completely or to ignore a disagreement. But we may want to consider the effects of our reactions and communicate at appropriate times our appreciation of the difficulty of having told the truth. We can add that we would have been much more upset if we had found out some other way. If we only fly into a rage, the primary response from the other person will be to avoid that reaction in the future. That probably means hiding things from us.

But lying is uncomfortable for most people; they would rather not lie if they sense there is another option. The possibility of getting caught and becoming branded as a liar makes lying unattractive. Dishonesty distances us from one another. Most of us would rather be accepted for who we are than for the lies we tell. Even in close relationships, there are reasons people are dishonest with one another. Strangers, being less trusting and also less accountable, feel even less constrained by the truth.

→ Consider that, among most people, empathy makes lying unnecessary.

Fortunately less common are the people who do not *mind* lying. For them, lying may be their first choice, and you may need to take a strident approach. It may be someone who constantly lies and undermines coworkers, or someone who is an outright con artist. These characters are beyond the reach of understanding. In those situations, we need to do more than say, "Don't lie." We need to deter the person from ever lying to us again by making it so painful for him to be caught in a lie that anything else is preferable. Our anger and disappointment are not enough. We may need to impose a penalty, as in a work situation, or share his deceit with others. Once the deceit becomes public knowledge, reputation is affected, and self-image is negatively altered. That is painful for most people. They will finally see a boundary that should not be crossed.

If you do forgive someone who has no compunctions about lying, do so silently. The value of forgiveness is to the forgiver, not to the incorrigible liar. To an unscrupulous person, forgiveness may be interpreted as implied permission to tell another lie as soon as the need arises.

During trials, it is common to challenge witnesses with their own pretrial testimony, when they may have made statements that were less calculated or coached than the testimony they present during the more formal setting of a trial. It is humiliating for a witness to hear his or her own contradictory statements read out loud. Most witnesses, after having their earlier statements read back to them a couple of times, are likely to stop taking liberties with the truth. I have been able to get witnesses to retract suspect statements merely by asking, "Are you sure?" while simultaneously reaching for their pretrial deposition transcript. Whether you do it through empathy, or by calling people on their lies publicly, you can eliminate many lies before they are told.

Choosing Appropriate Techniques

Women's magazines regularly feature articles on methods for detecting lies. With titles such as "How to Tell If He's Cheating on You," these articles sometimes conveniently assume the reader has the inclination to cross-examine any suspected liar and overtly express her suspicions.

Other articles and books on detecting liars go even further, describing techniques of law enforcement that could not possibly be used in social settings. In the world we live in, we may not have the freedom to even question, much less cross-examine or interrogate, a suspected liar.

You may, for example, be trying to figure out if your boss is lying to you. In a society where people have unequal power and want to maintain cordial relationships, we frequently find ourselves pretending to accept what we actually question, or even what we reject. Suspicion is seen as hostility or paranoia, so we spend a good deal of time biting our tongues. In some situations, you may have to rely on techniques that call upon your powers of observation rather than on trick questions or confrontations.

Technology

Technology does not yet offer any lie-detection miracles. While technology has demonstrated that there are some measurable physiological changes when a person lies, the main difficulty with various detection devices is that factors besides lying can also cause these changes. The polygraph, commonly known as the lie detector, measures physiological responses such as pulse, breathing rate, blood pressure, and skin conductivity during responses to questions. Does it work? Not infallibly; some estimates put its accuracy at around 60 percent, or only slightly better than chance. U.S. courts almost universally reject polygraph evidence. In California, polygraph evidence was specifically prohibited by the legislature in 1983.

The people who make money from administering polygraphs claim a success rate of more than 90 percent, although perhaps not while hooked up to their own machines.

People have been wrongly accused after volunteering to take a polygraph test when only their nervousness has been detected. Others can fool the machine. When I was a teenager, I knew someone who had gone out with a friend of his and damaged some road-building equipment. My acquaintance came under suspicion, denied responsibility, and was eventually given a lie detector test. Although completely guilty, he managed to pass the test by deliberately convincing himself it was the kid he was with who was really responsible. He proudly reported that he had repeated a phrase in his mind that condemned his friend each time he was asked a pertinent question. CIA spy Aldrich Ames and Green River killer Gary Ridgway also passed polygraph tests.[1] Falsehoods told by people who are not bothered by lying are difficult to detect, with or without a polygraph machine.

Controversy continues to surround the use of other technologies designed to reveal lies, such as voice-stress analysis and magnetic resonance imaging (MRI).[2] One type of MRI can show that the prefrontal cortex, the portion of the brain involved in reasoning, has to work harder when subjects are untruthful. Yet research has also shown there can be overlap between emotions other than those associated with lying.[3] The physiological mechanism of different *types* of lies may also show up differently on the MRI and thus be misinterpreted. Critics of the technology believe that lies involve multiple parts of the brain and that it is actually more difficult to see a lie being formulated in the brain than MRI proponents claim. Companies adapting the technology for commercial use have claimed high accuracy rates (such as 90 percent), but as of this writing, no court has ruled that the MRI is admissible evidence on the issue of veracity.

Other techniques have included analysis of brain waves and measuring micro-expressions on the face.[4] Sometimes drugs have been forcibly administered to elicit the truth. Although alcohol is not a truth serum, it is common knowledge that statements people would otherwise censor can follow a few drinks. This is especially the case with people who do not drink frequently and are unaccustomed to compensating for the effects.

Your Natural Advantage

If sophisticated medical technologies are not widely accepted methods for detecting lies, and if some people can fool at least the polygraph, what hope is there for human beings to detect the lies of others? Unlike a machine, we can formulate questions and strategies for discerning the truth depending on the circumstances. We can listen to tone of voice, intuitively compare it to the dozens of other tones of voice we have heard, watch facial expressions, observe body language, and check facts.

Pathological and professional liars may see lying as a challenge and the accumulation of successful lies as proof of their cleverness. Yet most of the lies we encounter are from ordinary people balancing their perceived need to lie against potential consequences. Unpracticed liars are uncomfortable with lying. If their lies are discovered, the people they have lied to will get mad and may try to get even. Worse, the liar can be permanently disgraced.

The average person will limit the frequency and scope of his lies as much as possible, even if sticking closer to the facts makes the lie less credible. If he is later found out, he would rather be known for having told a little lie than for laying out an elaborate web of deception. If lying a little is bad, lying a lot is much worse.

When someone seems to be trying to find out how much you already know about a subject, it may be a clue that she is sizing up the lie she feels the need to tell. She wants to shape the lie so it starts right where your knowledge ends but also to limit the territory the lie covers to only what is necessary. If a person asks, "Why do you want to know?" before answering a question, she may be trying to determine what would be hopeless to lie about and where her lie needs to begin and end. While questioning suspects, law enforcement personnel commonly pretend to have more information than they actually do. If they are convincing, the suspect feels trapped and divulges information he believes the police have anyway. A detective with a strong suspicion may falsely say,

"We know you were hanging around on Fourth Street that night." If the suspect was on Fourth Street on the night in question, he may admit that much rather than risk becoming a proven liar with no remaining possibility of talking his way out of the situation.

Signals of the Outright Lie

Entire books are dedicated to recognizing lies, others to reading body language. Yet while such analyses are worth studying, inflexible rules about liars are problematic. There are innumerable variables among liars in personality, regional and ethnic differences, gender, power dynamics, and age, as well as the contexts in which they lie. For example, one rule states that whenever someone says, "I'm going to be perfectly honest . . ." it signals that a lie is about to be told. Yet it might also signal that the speaker is about to say something blunt or painfully honest and is only preparing the listener for the shock. Rules and automatic assumptions about lying can get in the way of keeping an open mind. Your intelligence and life experiences are the most consistently reliable guides. If there were a set of rules that worked in every situation, there would be no successful liars.

Bear in mind that outright lies are only one aspect of the problem. Whatever a person says is either a characterization of what he believes to be true or a statement of what he believes to be untrue. Accurate or inaccurate information can be delivered in either circumstance, and falsehoods can unknowingly be spoken with sincere conviction.

Eye Contact

Another well-known rule is that liars avoid looking people in the eye. If you take this to heart and assume that everyone who looks you in the eye is telling you the truth, you will be successfully lied to. Although there are cultural differences, both too little *and* too much eye contact can be signs of a liar. Usually it is too little, but because everyone knows this, it is unreliable. For example, when I bought one of my first cars, the seller stared pointedly at me while she lied. When I first went to see the car, she could not get it started. That did not concern me very much because I had learned to work on cars, so I agreed to return a few days later. Before I arrived, the seller had somehow gotten the car warmed up (probably by push-starting it), so this time the engine fired up right away. But instead of coming clean, she told a ridiculous lie: "I was using the wrong damn key." As she said this, she looked at me so intently that more than thirty years later, I can still picture her expression.

The "wrong damn key" probably would not have fit into the ignition, much less turned and allowed the starter motor to crank the engine over. I was able to negotiate a good price because the seller believed there was something seriously wrong with the car. She was mistaken. Oddly, I became the liar, by omission, because I did not tell her the car needed only an ignition timing adjustment.

Body Language

It has been said that the body does not lie. Often, all we have to do is stop paying attention to ourselves long enough to appreciate what is visually obvious about others. You have no doubt seen poor performances by people who were disappointed when they opened a gift but struggled to appear pleased. Yet if you are the giver, your perceptions are going to be shaded by your own feelings, and you might have a harder time seeing the falsity of the performance. Part of you wants to believe in it. On the other hand, if you are able to focus on the other person and see a lack of spontaneity or hear a strained vocal tone, those clues will reveal the recipient's true feelings.

Or you may notice whether someone has her arms crossed, whether she is willing to sit or stand near you, and whether the muscles around her eyes are involved when she smiles. Although we stretch, yawn, and scratch for purely physiological reasons, our physical movements are mainly discretionary. How we place our arms, hands, and legs and tilt our heads all relate to our emotional state as well as to our physical comfort. Just as someone with a sore back may instinctively sit in a certain way to relieve pressure, people assume physical postures in response to emotional states. Even small movements that appear pointless are motivated by *something*. It may be physical discomfort, restlessness, irritation, fright, or attraction. While we cannot possibly analyze the meaning of every posture and gesture, some are more telling than others.

Yet apart from observing that someone is crossing his or her fingers while speaking, no single clue is definitive. We can pay close attention to the small signs, such as a person touching her face as an unconscious, protective move. When a hand covers the mouth, it may be an effort to hide emotion or restrain a statement. A person who is lying is especially unlikely to touch you. A leg crossed away from you can mean defensiveness. Lack of movement is also revealing; if someone seems to speak passionately but uses no gestures, it suggests a lack of conviction. Swallowing, clearing one's throat, and trembling are strong clues. Other suspect gestures include shrugs, hooking feet around furniture, or looking slightly to the left, as if telling the lie to an invisible companion. There may also be a vocal hint of false earnestness, a milder version of the hypersincerity we hear in TV and radio commercials.

Just after a person utters what you think may be a lie, notice whether he is watching you. Only a very good liar will have the confidence to look away, as though he simply does not care whether you just bought what he said. Most people will look for reassurance that they got away with something.

Working It from the Edges

Even when we have the freedom to play the role of interrogator and pepper someone with questions, it is not always the wisest approach. Being lied to is unpleasant, and confronting a suspected liar is also unpleasant. We may be tempted to get the scene over with quickly, or we may find ourselves venting anger about the lie or even about unrelated subjects. Unlike a professional interrogator whose feelings are relatively uninvolved, when we are demanding answers, our own emotions can quickly make a person more defensive than honest.

If we immediately demand an answer to the ultimate question we want answered, it will probably lead to the ultimate denial. Suppose a plumbing company allows one of its employees to drive a company truck home while the employee's car is being repaired. The employer gives strict instructions that the employee is not to use the truck for any purpose except driving to or from work. On Monday morning, the supervisor hears a rumor (that no one is willing to back up) that the employee was seen around town on Saturday night. He could ask the ultimate question: "Did you use the company truck to go out on Saturday night?" The employee might be brazen enough to say "No," at which point the conversation could be over.

Instead, while maintaining a nonjudgmental attitude to avoid putting the employee on the defensive, the supervisor might start a conversation that boxes the employee in, bit by bit. "How much longer is your car going to be in the shop?" Then, "Oh, you probably have to run errands like everybody else over the weekend. It must be a nuisance not to have a car," at which point the employee might allow that he did go to the grocery store. And then, "I guess you stopped by the Hotsie Totsie Club on Saturday night, too." If the employee was there, he may not want to risk of being caught telling a flat-out lie.

Speech and Generalities

Amateur liars do not like specifics. They do not like exact numbers, dates, times, or quantities. When they provide details, they have to remember them later. Fabrications are harder to remember than events that actually occurred because there is no visual, auditory, or tactile imagery for a liar to associate with fabrications. Each detail also provides a new avenue for checking up on the liar, and a cat sitting next to a rocking chair does not need any extra tails. Listen for words used to avoid specifics, such as "basically" and "generally." Pay attention to claimed lack of memory about detail. When someone answers a question by reframing it and giving a response on a slightly different topic, they are almost certainly hiding something.

Lack of substance behind what someone is saying is also revealed by the popular phrase, "You know what I mean?" It is not really a question but a statement. Most often, it suggests that the speaker herself is not entirely sure what she means and is hoping the listener is filling in gaps. It does not always signal a lie, although it usually does signal uncertainty.

Generalities are not to be confused with the normal, inexact speech we are all accustomed to hearing. The crisp dialogue of movies and television, with actors taking turns reciting complete, articulate sentences, does not come close to the dialogues of daily life. In reality, people often speak in fragments. Verbatim transcripts of interviews read like this:

Q: So, when did you first move in? The apartment?

A: I think it was, uh, that was when I had that Dodge. It was . . . no, let me think . . . 2006, 2007, maybe.

Q: Was it . . . who lived there with you?

A: Oh. First, I think . . . yeah. I moved in by myself for two . . . what was it? Might have been a month. Was that when Steve . . . ? Who was . . . all these different people wanted to, to move, but there . . . this one guy, Ted . . .

Q: Ted was . . . Sorry, go on.

Here the person being interviewed may not be trying to hide anything but is responding to questions in a normal, if inexact and mostly unresponsive, way. A liar is not likely to wander around so aimlessly, spilling unnecessary facts that might be used to check his story. He would rather get the essence of the lie told with at least some clarity so he can move on to something less stressful.

Less often, a brazen lie will be full of details, overselling the story. A truly sophisticated lie may even include some contradictions so the lie does not seem too perfect, with its lesser pieces seeming not to support the conclusion compelled by the larger ones. For example, a man selling a used car who knows the transmission is on its way out may talk about what a great car it is, then say, "I have to be honest with you. The radio isn't the best. Sometimes it cuts out for a few seconds when you're on a bumpy road."

It is difficult for people promoting anything of marginal value to resist hyping the item with "really," "very," "extremely," and so forth. Also listen for the stage-setting phrases liars use, such as, "This is going to sound strange . . ." People do not feel much need to editorialize about the truth. When we believe we are saying something that is true, we just say it.

Labels as Implicit Lies

When we label concepts, the particular words in the label may ultimately come to have more social and political clout than the underlying concept. Labels can be applied to groups of people. For instance, many liberals these days prefer to be called progressives. The meanings of the labels are essentially the same, but for decades, conservatives have used the phrase "tax-and-spend liberals" to denigrate their political opponents. By using a new word to describe themselves, liberals escape some of the negative connotations of the older label. For a time, George W. Bush adopted the old trick of referring to the Democratic Party as the "Democrat Party," out of apparent concern that "Democratic Party" implied that Republicans were not democratic. Some Republicans still refuse to call the opposing party by its correct name.

In the same way that advertising so effectively uses sexual innuendo to sell products that have nothing to do with sex, other incongruous concepts are often bundled together to create compelling associations. Just as advertisers place attractive models next to the products they're selling, issues can be tied together with language. One concept is tied to a different, emotionally loaded concept, using carefully chosen words as the twine. It is regularly done with hot-button issues such as taxes, religion, and abortion, but even more commonly in milder contexts. For example, a Realtor named Stone might use the slogan, "For rock-solid real estate services, call Tom Stone." While having the name Stone has nothing to do with professional ability, just by playing with words, Tom Stone can plant the suggestion that his name and performance are connected.

In 2007, after the price of copper soared, a mining company launched an effort to expand copper mining in Arizona. Local residents and environmentalists objected. As part of its pitch, the mining company pointed out that the United States imported approximately half of the copper it used. The company stated that this country had a dependence on foreign copper just as it had a dependence on foreign oil.[5] For people in the United States, dependence on foreign oil carries a distinctly negative connotation. When oil prices go up, the effect at the pump is real and immediate. Consumers who lived through the oil crisis of the 1970s remember how a shortage created horrendous lines at gas stations, high prices, and difficulty finding gasoline at all. People remain aware of instability in the Middle East and its potential effect for disruptions to the world oil supply. By pairing foreign copper with foreign oil, the mining company hoped to create a connection to an existing concept. Yet the reality is that while a sudden scarcity of foreign copper would have negative effects on the United States, it would not create the same magnitude of crisis as a scarcity of oil.

Different moods can be evoked by selecting one word instead of another: "inexpensive" instead of "cheap," "pre-owned" in place of "used," "expedited" for "rushed," "discerning" for "fussy," or "discreet" where "sneaky" might be more accurate. Positive connotations can be manufactured by finding ways to inject warm, fuzzy words such as "family" or "cozy." Conversely, negative connotations can be created by finding a way to include words that trigger unpleasant associations, such as "divorce" or "molest."

Sophisticated or well-coached witnesses use linguistic and conceptual tricks when testifying; lawyers and others use them when arguing. Speechwriters and salespeople are well aware of the power of connotations and concepts and are experts in exploiting it.

The Implicit Liar

An implicit liar advances a hidden agenda by using the powers of suggestion and connotation rather than by uttering outright false statements. It is a tactic used most often when the subtext would sound preposterous, such as announcing during a meeting, "I am a great man." Instead, the "great man" lets you know all about his accomplishments, his cleverness, his conquests, the famous people he knows, and the adulation he receives from others. He reveals nothing about his business failures, the children he abandoned, or the motorcycle accident he was in after a night of heavy drinking. He gives his audience information only to piece together the conclusion, "He must be a great man."

This person, who might also be called a manipulator, may lie in a complimentary fashion, most commonly with the flattery that comes easily to those who want something but cannot ask for it directly. Such people can be highly destructive. Individuals who provide us with selective information pointing to a specific conclusion—whether they are egotists or narcissists or are merely advancing a financial, political, or romantic goal—are best avoided. Their selective presentations would be unnecessary if they did not have a purpose at odds with your interests.

Whatever their agenda, implicit liars probably spent years developing skill at building false impressions and making them difficult to spot. They may not only be practiced at hiding their underlying agenda but may give us reasons to want to believe what they say.

Some signs of implicit lies are:

- Implicit liars put energy into making others feel a certain way. Much of what they do and say is for its calculated effect. They may strive to make you feel important and desirable, or undesirable and incompetent, but the common denominator is that these people are at work pushing your buttons. Interactions with them can have a somewhat strained feel, although you may not be able to say why. They avoid making any statements that actually characterize what they present; the responsibility for making any characterizations is left to you.
- Implicit liars can make you feel unusually special, unusually liked, unusually agitated, or unusually awful about yourself. The ideas and emotions generated are not likely to feel familiar. You may start feeling better about yourself or questioning yourself more than is typical for you, because of what they say.
- The motivations of the implicit liar can remain hidden for as long as you do not want to recognize them. While someone is flattering you, it is harder to see that what she really wants is your money or your acquiescence.
- Implicit liars may have a keen sense of what you think or feel and make use of that. If you are proud of certain accomplishments, implicit liars may talk about them. If they are trying to discourage you, they may concentrate on the things you feel most sensitive about.
- Although implicit liars are masters of flattery, they do not generate true loyalty. Just like outright liars, they put a false spin on reality for selfish purposes, and people sense it. Others may pretend to like them and may even be afraid to criticize them in private. But you are not likely to hear other people volunteering positive comments about an implicit liar.

Sometimes there is little choice but to deal with an implicit liar. He may be a guest seated next to you at a dinner party, or the person sharing a cubicle with you. The most effective thing to do is to let him know immediately that you are on to him. Even statements as basic as "You're just trying to flatter me" or "You're just trying to make me feel bad" will have an effect. The effect will not be visible—the manipulator will deny it and accuse you of being overly suspicious, and he may pretend to be offended, but he will also know you are right. You may need to go through the exercise several times, finding different language each time. But you have an advantage; the implicit liar's big fear is having his true motivations revealed. He lives with the knowledge that being manipulative rather than straightforward is undesirable. Each time you reach behind the small truths he offers and mention the larger implicit lie he is telling, you threaten his disguise. When he senses you can see right through him, he is going to treat you more carefully, if not with more respect.

The well-crafted implicit lies of criminals, politicians, corporations, and advertisers are designed with extreme care, using selective language to give the untrue or improbable both emotional weight and credibility. Words can carry suggested truths beyond their dictionary definitions, evoking moods, connotations, and images that do not accurately reflect reality.

By the fall of 2009, the green movement was in full swing as a social phenomenon; in some circles it had taken on the authority of a social imperative. Manufacturers and their advertisers had found methods for hooking into the trend. The November 2, 2009, issue of *The New Yorker* magazine carried a full-page ad for a faucet manufacturer claiming that a line of its household faucets had a flow rate that saved up to 32 percent more water per minute—described as a flow rate of 1.5 gpm versus an industry standard of 2.2 gpm.[6] The suggestion was that purchasers would be doing the earth a favor by buying this special faucet, even though they could achieve the identical result by not opening their existing faucets all the way. The same issue carried a full-page ad for a hybrid car. In the background was a whimsical tree formed out of tightly clustered humans wearing brown-and-green clothing. The ad claimed the car delivered more power and had lower emissions. The connotation was that you were either part of the cluster of humanity that formed the tree, and part of the green movement, or you were an outsider.

What Poker Players Know

Experienced poker players hide their emotions and sometimes win pots by bluffing as they pretend to hold cards different from those actually in their hands. They lie by implication with the size of their bets and assess whether other players are trying the same thing. Sophisticated players interpret any display of emotion as deliberate; supposed confidence indicates a weak hand, while timidity suggests a strong one. Most clues are subtle. Players watch one another for small changes in body language and may be able to sense where the other players hold tension in their bodies. They may then detect when that tension is released, indicating a shift in mood. Breathing rates can be discerned, and in fact any change in behavior is a clue—such as when a fidgety person becomes calm or a calm person fidgety. Players may take drinks more or less frequently depending on their state of mind. A good player may recognize a "tell," an automatic movement, such as touching the back of the neck, as a sign of discomfort, or watch for other players to touch their chips when they are dealt a good hand.

Because poker is a game that has a start and a finish as well as an obvious goal, players are able to maintain their high level of scrutiny; they can relax after the game. Not all everyday situations have such clear beginnings and endings, so we must decide when it is important to pay close attention. One clue is unusual behavior. If you notice any behavior that telegraphs deception from a person you deal with regularly, just make a mental note. If you mention it to her, she will of course deny it, resent it, and take care not to display it to you again.

Tools for Specific Transactions: Con Games

In 2007, the Federal Trade Commission issued a report on the results of a survey indicating that more than 30 million Americans were victimized by consumer fraud in 2004.[7] These people participated in the fraud to various degrees, from merely having a credit card to responding to ridiculous Internet schemes offering something for nothing.

Classic Con Games

Con games promise huge rewards for an investment that is never returned. The victim participates purely because of the confidence he places in the swindler. Schemes may have a veneer of respectability and may provide a participant with a feeling of being important or charitable. Frequently, victims do not complain to authorities because their participation has drawn them into illegal acts, or they are ashamed of their naivety.

Pyramid schemes operate by recruiting new members ostensibly to sell a product or service. Compensation is dependent on recruiting new members and moving higher up the chain. The promoters proclaim that their enterprise is all about selling a product and insist, "It's not a pyramid scheme!" But the compensation schedule always bears a curious resemblance to a pyramid, with those who get in early reaping large benefits and those who get in at the end losing everything.

When Bernie Madoff was arrested in 2009 for bilking investors out of billions of dollars, we heard on the news that it was a Ponzi scheme. This style of fraud is named after Charles Ponzi, who operated in the 1920s, promising a 50 percent return on money within two or three months. Ponzi claimed to be able to make money investing in postal-reply coupons. By actually paying the first investors high return rates, he was able to attract others, but because there was no money actually being invested and the money from new investors was used to pay off old investors, his scheme eventually collapsed. Ponzi was arrested for fraud.

The version of the pyramid scheme you are most likely to see is in the form of an invitation to become involved in a direct-marketing program. These organizations sell products not available in stores. They make significant money by recruiting new members; sales of the product are much less significant. Such schemes are not necessarily illegal, but their main effect is to generate income for the people who buy in early.

Your Front Door

A swindler may ring doorbells posing as a utility company representative, contractor, city official, building inspector, or neighbor. Or he may claim that someone has had an emergency and needs money or that there is a neighborhood problem that requires financial support. Whatever form it takes, he makes up a lie and collects money by catching people off guard.

Your Internet Connection

You have probably received e-mails from people you do not know asking for your assistance in transferring a large amount of money to the United States. If you respond, you are then told you have to provide funds in order to free up a gigantic amount of money. You are offered a huge percentage in exchange for your help. Sometimes you are asked repeatedly for money after being told of delays and problems, until you finally balk. Of course, the only money actually involved is what you send the people running the scam.

In another scheme, the victim is told he can make money helping collect debts. Stolen checks are mailed to him with his name as payee. The victim is instructed to cash the checks and return most of the money to the con artist. The person cashing the check is then on the hook for any reimbursement due to the check writer, and he may face criminal prosecution.

All kinds of things are offered for sale on the Internet—drugs, guns, pirated software. Because the victim usually knows she is trying to buy something illegally, she is less likely to complain when the drugs turn out to be sugar pills, the gun is a plastic toy, or the software does not work—if the item arrives at all. Even if the victim complains, the seller may be impossible to find.

The scam known as "phishing" operates a little differently. It takes advantage not of the victim's greed but of his motivation to play by the rules. Here, the swindler sends an e-mail supposedly from a company with which the victim has an account, such as a bank. The e-mail advises the victim that as a security precaution, or for account reactivation or other routine activity, he must verify his personal information on a Web site. The link in the e-mail takes the victim to a pirate site, outfitted with official-looking logos to appear legitimate. The victim voluntarily plugs in credit card numbers and other information useful to an identity thief. Most people recognize these attempts at fraud, but because the messages are sent out by the hundreds of thousands, a small percentage of people are taken in.

As you can imagine, new Internet schemes are invented every day.

On the Street

One type of street con involves people who set up a van in a parking lot, pretending to be employees of an electronics store who just discovered that they have, for example, an extra stereo or set of speakers the store forgot to catalog in its inventory. The boxed equipment is said to be worth thousands of dollars but is available for just a few hundred. When the victim forks over the cash and takes the sealed boxes home, he finds he has purchased low-quality or broken equipment or sometimes just some bricks. He is not in a position to complain that his attempt to purchase stolen goods did not work out.

Not Quite True

Nearly all con games make use of the victim's own greed as the trap. Illegal cons have milder, legal forms, but they are based on the same principle that people are eager to get something for nothing. Stores sometimes use "bait and switch" tactics that lure people in with the promise of a bargain. The bargain item, the clerk tells them, is unfortunately sold out, but there is a comparable, more expensive item in stock. Other stores have perpetual "Going Out of Business" sales.

Restaurants hardly need to encourage their servers, whose income is largely from tips, to run up customers' bills as high as they can. Sometimes the servers do not serve water unless the customer asks, in the hope that the customer will at least order mineral water. There is tremendous markup in restaurants on any drink that contains alcohol. Servers love to describe how good the appetizers and desserts are. They frequently describe dinner specials without mentioning their higher prices. Once a skilled server takes control of the transaction, customers may feel deserving of the extras and may feel like cheapskates if they turn them down.

Marketing gimmicks are endless. One, seen on the ingredients listing of many fruit-flavored drinks, shows the first ingredient as "filtered water." *All* water is filtered, if only by the municipality that supplied the water to the beverage-processing plant. Adding the word *filtered* is supposed to make the consumer pay less attention to the fact that the main ingredient in the juice drink is water. (The next ingredient is often high-fructose corn syrup, followed by "juice from concentrate.") Sometimes several different types of sugars are used, making it less obvious from the label just how much total sugar is in the product. Marketers come up with cute names for these products, rather than more honestly calling them "fruit-flavored sugar-water." The public might not buy them if they did.

Legal forms of chiseling rely on misleading or suggestive labeling, pride, and consumers' reluctance to return items for refunds. We may feel embarrassed to assert our right to get our money's worth. Petty chiselers profit from exploiting our vulnerabilities.

Contractors: Whom to Trust?

Consumers are taken advantage of every day. Sometimes misrepresentations are blatant: a supposed contractor accepts a large deposit for a new roof and then disappears. Or the fraud is more subtle—the contractor charges for work properly done but unnecessary, charges for necessary work done poorly, or charges significantly more than the competition. When the main concern is getting the job done, we may be tempted to rely on intuition or on a single recommendation. Yet because the price of a mistake can be significant, it is worthwhile to put aside any sense of urgency, obtain and check references, search for complaints with the Better Business Bureau, review license status and disciplinary actions by licensing boards, and, where possible, look at examples of the person's past work. Plugging the name of a person or business into an Internet search engine may yield results, although it is important to be certain any references that come up are really to the intended target. Also, comments found on the Internet may not have been screened; they may be accurate, but they may also be completely unfair.

Direct questions can work wonders in bringing the truth to the surface. You can phrase such questions in ways that do not make you seem hostile or suspicious:

- *How many times have you done this work before?* The contractor will not be able to give you an exact number, but if he is not comfortable with an estimate (dozens, hundreds), he may still be learning—at your expense. His response should be automatic; the question should not make him uncomfortable. If he says in a slightly unfriendly tone, "I don't know the *exact* number," he is playing with words rather than trying to be cooperative.

- *Are there less-expensive options?* This deserves a straightforward response and should not create any discomfort either. There is usually a cheaper way to do just about anything, although a cheaper method may not be advisable.
- *Are there more-expensive options I should consider?* This is not just a trick to see if the person will try to sell you something you do not need. If there are more expensive solutions to the problem, there is a greater likelihood that you have already been offered the most economical solution.
- *Do you know what your competition is charging?* Of course the contractor knows. A typical response is, "Our prices are in line with everyone else's." Because you can verify this objectively by getting other bids, you can verify whether the contractor is being honest with you.
- *Do you think you are the right one for this job?* An automatic "yes" is not the answer you are looking for. A skilled, honest person who is in demand will explain your options and may even refer you to others. This may be where you find out whether the bidder has your interests in mind or his own. Someone who offers glib assurances that he is better than everyone else is not likely to make your concerns a priority.

Truth in Dating

Few situations demand as much quick lie detection, or have such direct emotional consequences, as dating. Blunt questions at an early stage of dating may be inappropriate, calling on us to use intuition to detect deception and perceive subtle clues.

People sell themselves to others by displaying their best traits while hiding and finessing their worst. Because we hope that a date actually has all the wonderful qualities she advertises, wishful thinking can get in the way of seeing the whole picture. Dating presents continual choices between accepting what is presented or turning over rocks. Regardless of what we do, the truth will unfold eventually.

→ To speed up the process, there are several factors you can consider:

- *Appearance.* The more physically attractive the person is, the more you are blinded. It is that simple. As when you are driving into the sun, it is hard to see where you are going. Remind yourself of this again and again. When your friends comment on your date's attractiveness, remind yourself again. When you say, "It doesn't affect my judgment!" remind yourself again. There is nothing inherently wrong with good-looking people. But the fact that you find a person attractive does not necessarily make that person a good match.
- *History.* People either have a dating history or a telling lack of dating experience. Although I do not recommend it for a first date, subtly encouraging a person to talk about prior relationships and listening in a nonjudgmental way can yield a wealth of information. Listen carefully; this is how he may be talking about you someday. You may learn why past relationships ended or sense that your date does not fully understand why. He may relate only a mixture of reactions and characterizations. Someone who understands and admits he made a mistake is more perceptive than someone who provides only reasons why nothing was his own fault or just seems baffled when asked what went wrong.
- *Energy.* The point of an initial date is to find out more about a person and, one hopes, to have some fun in the process. But if your date spends energy emphasizing her good points, complaining, or talking about celebrities, television, or the boring details of her job, she is neither helping you have a good time nor trying to find out more about you. If there is no genuine curiosity about you now, is there ever going to be any? You are selling yourself short if you tell yourself such lack of interest is okay.

- *Money.* A man's insistence on paying for a meal may seem nice and can make his date feel valued, but his gesture could also be symbolic of his intention to use money as a way to exert control. A woman's expectation that the man will pull out his wallet may seem to offer him the opportunity to be a gentleman, while it may also be a message that she is doing him a favor by going out with him or that her belief in gender equality has limits.
- *Lies.* If you can tell, or you even strongly suspect, that your date is lying about something, remember how unlikely it is to get any better as the relationship progresses. Lying is how that person deals with stress or feelings of inadequacy. Your date may be good looking, funny, or rich, but this is someone who can also make you miserable. His emotional needs may always take priority over your desire to know the truth. Try to understand the reason for the lie, but take it as a strong warning sign.

The Truth Is Yours If You Want It

Much of what is presented to us as fact is only an amalgam of selected truths, opinions, guesses, and/or lies. Although we are surrounded by inaccurate representations, we do not need to be controlled by them. Recognizing inaccuracies requires knowledge of the common traits and motivations of liars, but even more than following any set of rules, it means paying attention. Recognizing lies often requires a willingness to question those things you would rather accept at face value.

Your recognition of lies will be unwelcome, whether you question representations overtly or silently via your attitude. Standing your ground and discovering the truth, whether loudly or quietly, may require considerable courage. It is worthwhile. Like old paint, falsity scrapes off readily enough, and the underlying truth will be far more useful to you. Never give up your right to determine the truth for yourself. No one should be at the mercy of others' false representations.

6

←————————→

Lessons from Science

U nderstanding some basic principles of science can help you in many ways. If you are nervous about flying, you may be reassured if you learn about aerodynamics and discover there are good reasons why a plane stays in the sky; learning and applying principles of nutrition will help you feel better and avoid disease; understanding soil types and plant fertilizers makes you a more competent gardener; and knowing how different cleaning products function allows you to choose the best one for the job.

Good science reveals how and why processes work. Science uses a systematic method of experimentation and analysis. With the insights it provides, science allows us to cure illnesses, predict hurricanes, cook with microwaves, and communicate wirelessly. By keeping in mind what is scientific and what is not, you can also avoid becoming a victim of pseudoscientific marketing claims about products of all types. Before examining detailed applications of science to your life, a look at the basic tools of scientific reasoning will be helpful.

Deductive Logic

Since the time of Aristotle (384–322 BCE), deductive logic has been used as a reasoning process.[1] Here is an example:

1. All dogs are canines (a generalized statement generally agreed to be an objective truth).

2. My pet, Lucy, is a dog.

3. Therefore, Lucy is a canine.

Deductive logic can also be expressed as an abstract formula:

1. $A = B$.

2. $C = A$.

3. Therefore, $C = B$.

Inductive Logic

Also called inductive reasoning, the arguments of inductive logic move from the general to the particular.[2] That is, an observation is made, and no facts are found to contradict it. The conclusion is applied to particular situations until the observation is proven wrong. Inductive logic calls for some caution, although we all use it in daily life. For example, you are driving a car and approach an intersection with a four-way stop. At the same time, a bicyclist is approaching the intersection from the left. You make an assumption that the bicyclist will run the stop sign, because you have seen hundreds of bicyclists run stop signs. You have not seen this particular bicyclist run this particular stop sign before, but you apply your general observation to the specific situation.

The Scientific Method

The scientific method evolved over hundreds of years. The widely accepted method used today is a series of steps.[3] You may have been taught the steps with some variation (scientists argue about precisely how each should be defined),[4] but essentially, they are:

1. *Observation.* The scientist makes an observation, then asks a question about it. She must then carry out initial research to see if the question has already been answered or if any existing experiments suggest how further experimentation might best be carried out.

2. *Hypothesis.* The hypothesis is the experimenter's belief about what has been observed. It might be as vague as an intuitive hunch or as precise as a prediction based on a mathematical model. If the belief holds up after experimentation, it may become accepted as support for a theory. However, while a hypothesis can be disproved, it can never be proved with absolute certainty.

3. *Experiment.* The experiment is designed to see if it disproves the hypothesis, and it must be carefully structured if its results are to be valid. Variables must be controlled; often this is done using a control group similar to an affected group but not subjected to the conditions that form the basis for the experiment. For example, an experiment might test different crop varieties with different fertilizers in different soils to see which combinations perform best. For each crop tested in a particular soil type, one group of plants would be grown using a fertilizer, and one without it for comparison.

4. *Analyzing the data.* In the above example, the scientist then looks at the data she has gathered to compare results. She uses statistical methods to assess the probability that differing results between the groups were due to chance. If the hypothesis states that a particular fertilizer in a particular soil type will produce the highest crop yield, this outcome would be supported by higher yield measurements in that group. If the conditions did not have the anticipated effect, the hypothesis is disproved. The researcher might then formulate a revised hypothesis and start again.

5. *Conclusion and communication.* Once the results of an experiment are substantiated, they are articulated and shared with others. Publication of an experiment in a scientific journal subjects the results to scrutiny, first by the journal's editors and peer reviewers, then by its readership. If the experiment is well designed, others should be able to carry it out and obtain the same results. An experiment flawed in design or execution is problematic; the results may suggest that a hypothesis should be accepted when it is actually invalid. This can lead to pointless efforts to duplicate the result, or worse, reliance on the flawed experiment without further testing. In experiments of lesser importance, results may go unexamined.

Limitations of the Scientific Method

An appropriate hypothesis is at the core of a good experiment. It does not spring from the absolute unknown but from a tentative conclusion based on initial observation. If a hypothesis is too conservative, the experiment teaches nothing except to confirm the obvious; time and money are wasted. If a hypothesis is too speculative, an experiment is not likely to support it. Yet if no one dares to test possibilities, no discoveries are made.

Historically, deficient experimentation was a huge obstacle to scientific progress. Incorrect assumptions, a lack of rigorous methods, and the scarcity of financial resources prevented untold numbers of possible experiments from being carried out. But the biggest obstacle was the lack of accurate tools with which to verify hypotheses and assumptions. Without good microscopes, people had a much harder time understanding biological processes. When there were no ships that could travel between continents with compasses and accurate mapping tools, the apparent flatness of the earth seemed perfectly logical using the only tool available, visual perception of the horizon. Long before it was understood that bats use sound to navigate, people were baffled by the apparent ability of bats to see in the dark; vision was all that was understood at the time.

Without tools for determining what is actually occurring, we are prone to state theory as fact and propose elaborate mythologies when it would be more honest and accurate to admit a lack of understanding. We tend to create myths in the social and political worlds as well as in the physical world, but the physical world is subject to concrete tests that are somewhat more definitive than those in the social realm.

Still, science is not exact or absolute; even the simplest scientific statements are subject to exception, variation, and abbreviation. For example, because *pi* has been calculated to more than 2 trillion digits, scientists and mathematicians must use a rounded figure and accept an approximate result. Water boils at a lower temperature at sea level than at ten thousand feet, and the precise structure of each person's DNA is different from that of others. The presence of variables, including those scientists are not yet aware of, is one of the reasons scientific progress is sometimes slow.

The progress of science is also impeded by its imperfect interface with human behavior and everyday intuition. For example, what are the odds of a coin toss coming up tails after nine flips that were heads? The answer is exactly 50–50, just as with the other nine; and while we may accept that, it is hard not to expect to finally see tails on the tenth flip. Medical science tells us with some certainty what is unhealthy, but people still eat salty and fatty foods, fail to exercise, drink too much alcohol, and engage in risky physical behaviors. Applying the truths of medical science to improve health is more effective if coupled with an understanding of the subjective experiences of people who jeopardize their health.

It is easy to point to the adverse effects of cigarette smoking and declare that people should not smoke. The health hazards are no longer a secret, yet an estimated 46 million people in the United States, or 20.6 percent of all adults ages eighteen years and older, smoke cigarettes.[5] The logical argument about the health dangers of smoking clearly has failed to persuade one person out of five to quit. Nor does that argument take into account whatever sedative effects nicotine has on anxious people. The logical argument misses the subjective experience of addiction and the satisfaction smokers experience when they quench a physical craving. The logical argument misses that many times during the course of a day, a smoker develops an urge, satisfies that urge with wonderfully predictable success, and then repeats the cycle. The logical argument misses the fact that the majority of smokers *enjoy* smoking. Moreover, sometimes smokers fear the effects of quitting more than the effects of continuing to smoke. Many people do not quit because they believe they will automatically gain weight. Some smokers may be more afraid of getting fat than of the harmful effects of smoking.

Even among scientists, good science is subject to misinterpretation and misrepresentation. Pride can be an issue. FBI examiners concluded that a fingerprint associated with the March 2004 Madrid train bombing belonged to an Oregon attorney; investigators in Spain disagreed. The FBI stood by its conclusions at great personal cost to the accused and was forced to apologize when the suspect was found to be innocent.[6] In other forensic tests, DNA analysis can be done improperly, and causes of death can be improperly attributed to foul play.[7]

The Randomness of Scientific Discovery

Science has illuminated the workings of biology, botany, chemistry, physics, and its other branches, creating medical techniques and devices for our comfort such as electric lights and air conditioning. With all that science has given us, it is easy to overlook the ways in which scientific progress has always staggered rather than marched forward. Scientific discovery is an ever-evolving process; science answers some questions, while simultaneously raising new ones. Advances can occur in bursts: rapid development of radar technology, the jet engine, and atomic energy were all motivated by the immediacy of the Second World War. Today, we move toward new energy technologies only as it becomes increasingly evident that our oil supplies will not last indefinitely and that greenhouse gases are adversely affecting the planet. Interest in new energy technologies rises even more when gasoline prices spike. Without motivation and funding, potential areas of research sit unexplored. Our scientific progress is something like exploring an unfamiliar building by flashlight: we place the beam of light where we think it will help us place our next step, not necessarily where the light will reveal the overall structure of the building.

Science does not exist without a community to teach its methods and critique the work of its members. Scientists who are not careful run the risk of embarrassing themselves. For example, Martin Fleischmann and Stanley Pons reported the exciting results of a cold-fusion experiment in 1989.[8] These experimenters believed that cold fusion held the promise of being a source of clean energy. They announced their findings at a press conference rather than waiting for publication in a scientific journal. When the results first came out, one scientific commentator was asked to compare the significance of the findings to another discovery. He replied, "Fire." But other scientists could not reproduce Fleischmann and Pons's findings. Both men ended up leaving the United States in disgrace; Pons went to France, and Fleischmann to England.

Huston Smith, a scholar of world religions and author of numerous books on the subject, observed that scientific discoveries can imply that whatever science has not discovered is not worthwhile. That would be an unfortunate assumption. If there are phenomena we have not yet been able to detect, their existence is not necessarily ruled out, and those phenomena certainly may be worthwhile to know about. Serious experimentation with radio waves did not get underway until the late 1800s.[9] Although radio and later television revolutionized communications by making information simultaneously available all over the globe, electromagnetic waves were not understood, let alone effectively harnessed, until relatively recently.

We almost certainly have comparable areas of ignorance today. While the principle that we do not know what we do not know can lead to funding for pure research, the principle also encourages pure speculation. The concept that there are unknowns, such as undiscovered types of matter or energy, is taken by some fringe thinkers as license to declare the existence of what they imagine. Poorly conducted experiments framed as science go a step farther by providing purported evidence for false conclusions.

As recently as the late eighteenth century, alchemists hunted for ways to turn lead into gold. The thrust of their endeavor was not to prove the process was possible but to acquire imagined riches. Phrenologists in the 1800s believed that the bumps on a person's head revealed his or her personality traits. More recently, iridologists believed (and some still do) that the specks in people's irises disclosed the presence of certain diseases.[10] Each of these, and dozens of other practices, have been examined and debunked as imaginative thinking or outright fraud masquerading as science.

While science may bring us closer than any other discipline to objective truth, many scientific discoveries are narrow. Science tends to shine its light on one subject, then another; we can cure some diseases but not others. We can harness energy using nuclear fission but not nuclear fusion. Areas of knowledge are scattered, as though we are looking through an observation window in a wall surrounding a construction site. By looking through the right portal at the right time, we may get a glimpse of something meaningful. At another moment, the physical world we see through the portals may appear to be chaotic. The physical world is always changing and may never be seen in its entirety even through a thousand portals or even if we remove the perimeter walls entirely. It is too much to ask that science deliver a view of all objective truth in which everything in the universe is explained.

Scientific research—and thus what we end up learning about the world around us—is heavily influenced by the practicalities of funding and the politics behind the funding. The reality is that research into a certain disease may receive government money solely because a congressperson's son or a celebrity's daughter happens to be afflicted with that particular ailment.

California State Senator Carole Migden fought a form of leukemia for years. After becoming cancer-free, she proposed a state system for collecting umbilical-cord blood, because cord blood was believed to play a potentially significant role in leukemia treatment.[11] Conversely, stem cell research received very limited support under the George W. Bush administration because of his religious convictions.[12] The highly personal truths of these politicians made real differences, both positive and negative, in other peoples' lives.

Scientific progress is also erratic because the scientific community changes its collective mind as new discoveries are made, contradicting prior beliefs. We might first hear that eating fish with omega-3 fatty acids can protect us from all heart ailments. Then a study comes along indicating that, except for a subgroup of people with diabetes, fish intake does not protect against heart failure in people without a history of coronary disease. (Fish intake appears to protect against heart attack but not heart failure.)[13] For years, we heard that coffee was bad for us; then we were told that coffee has some beneficial properties.

Prior to 2004, archaeologists commonly believed that humans first lived in North America some thirteen thousand years ago. Then Albert Goodyear, an archaeologist with the University of South Carolina, made a startling find near the Savannah River in South Carolina based on flint shards his team discovered. He concluded that humans had been on the continent for some *fifty thousand* years.[14] Thirty-seven thousand years of history is a significant chunk of time to be thrown in doubt, and conclusions such as Goodyear's call in question how much faith we should have in scientific theories, especially those about phenomena that are difficult to measure.

Nor are new developments in scientific discovery always welcome, even in the scientific community. In the first part of the twentieth century, geologists laughed at Alfred Wegener when he proposed the theory of continental drift, which suggested that the earth's continents had once all been connected.[15] Albert Einstein, while still a student at the Federal Polytechnic Institute in Zurich, questioned his professors when he thought they accepted existing theories of physics too easily.[16] They saw him as disrespectful and later made it difficult for him to get a teaching position. He was ostracized because he asked his professors to take a closer look at the truth. Einstein's questions threatened existing authority, which apparently mattered to his professors more than new discoveries.

However, Albert Einstein's break from academia turned out to give him more freedom. In his own words, "An academic career in which a person is forced to produce scientific writings in great amounts creates a danger of intellectual superficiality." Indeed, those who teach in academic institutions are under pressure to publish their work. Publishing truly novel or controversial work is risky, because it is less likely to be accepted by peers. One may be challenged for embracing new theories. No matter how valid, new beliefs that necessarily displace old beliefs threaten the authority of those whose dignity and authority depends on old ways of thinking. Intriguing conclusions within the confines of established thought are far safer.

Einstein pressed on; in 1906 he wrote six papers, and in 1907 he wrote ten. He was hired at the University of Zurich in May 1909, then at the University of Prague. When Einstein's hypothesis that light bends as it travels through space was successfully tested during a solar eclipse in May 1919, his discovery was recognized as true and revolutionary. Although Einstein eventually articulated some of the most profound truths about the universe that we know today, it is worth remembering that in the scientific community, he was initially treated not as a genius but as an annoyance.

The Mere Appearance of Scientific Method

We have all made decisions that turned out to be mistakes. You may have become convinced you knew what component failed in an automobile, appliance, or computer and then discovered that replacing the component did not solve the problem. Ordinary people and undisciplined scientists can fall into the trap of assuming a hypothesis is correct. We can fall in love with an idea and assume that idea is all we need, but a hypothesis alone is not the final word in science.

A distinctly unscientific method of interpretation is to develop a hypothesis, then look for existing evidence to support it. Radio talk-show hosts are fond of doing this; they present opinions as facts, then cite one or two isolated incidents as proof. They compensate for limited proof with displays of moral outrage. The radio host might, for instance, refer to a murderer who was released from prison on parole only to kill again and conclude that no killer should ever be allowed out of jail. Or the host might report the story of an undocumented immigrant who committed arson and proclaim that all undocumented immigrants should be deported. But one difference between a genuine experiment and a mere effort to justify an opinion is that the scientist will change a hypothesis if it is not validated by test results; the pundit will merely look for examples until he finds one that seems to prove his point.

Not all scientific theories are, or can be, tested immediately, due to a lack of appropriate technology, lack of funding, or general disinterest. But a theory can become accepted in the scientific community even without appropriate testing. For example, primate researchers were long puzzled about the vocal calls made by female chimpanzees while they were copulating, because making noise of any kind would reveal the chimps' location to predators. Biologists speculated that a female's calls were intended to attract other male partners so that the healthiest males would be competing to fertilize her egg. Yet a study of three hundred chimpanzee copulations in Uganda by Simon Townsend, Tobias Deschner, and Klaus Zuberbuhler showed that in two-thirds of the encounters, the females made no sound at all.[17] Thus, until the number of occasions when females made sounds was actually quantified, observers seem to have paid more attention to the calls they *did* hear (presumably a third of the time) than the occasions when there were no calls. Perhaps the earlier observers were alerted by the sounds, but they incorrectly assumed calls to be a standard component of chimpanzee copulation.

They then figured that the calls must have a specific evolutionary purpose and further speculated about the nature of that purpose. As it turns out, if the Uganda study is an accurate representation, the calls were actually more aberrational than standard. It is unclear why the assumptions and speculations of previous researchers were accepted. Possibly the unquestioning acceptance of the original chimp observations reflects some prudishness about examining sexual activity too closely. (Human vocalization during intercourse still remains poorly studied.) In any event, in the case of the chimps, the assumptions the researchers made were accepted without serious study. Theories are not necessarily scientific merely because they originate with scientists.

Junk Science

Superficial claims of scientific methodology can be misleading, even fraudulent. Ads may declare, "More doctors recommend XYZ medications" or "A leading survey found that ABC laundry detergent is superior." These meaningless phrases have nothing to do with real science. Statistics are particularly susceptible to misuse.[18] One could, for example, accurately state that the average annual income in a particular city is $110,000, if half its residents make $200,000, half make $20,000, and nobody makes anything in between. Reciting the average annual temperature or rainfall in a location can be just as misleading; a climate can be dry and hot in the summer and snowy and freezing in the winter, with no nice days at all. Rather than identifying the average annual temperature in a city, it would be more informative to identify the number of days in a year that the climate is within 10 degrees of 70 degrees Fahrenheit.[19]

Numbers can also be misused by offering supposedly representative samples that are so small they skew the results. Or numbers may be presented with no meaningful reference point, as in advertising. "Save 30 percent!" Thirty per cent of *what*? Numbers imply certainty, but unless we know what they truly represent and how they were derived, they can be misleading.

All too often, scientific studies are funded by the very industries whose products are being evaluated. Conflict of interest is inherent in such studies, and the necessarily questionable results should be viewed with skepticism. There are always people with advanced degrees who are willing to say what somebody wants them to. It is ultimately up to you to determine whether they have the science to back it up.

Chains of Causation

Understanding cause and effect helps us predict and control the future by showing what will happen if we set certain processes in motion. Science can explain many of the variables involved in causation. For instance, even with an act as simple as boiling water, using containers with varying densities will affect how long the process takes. Without clear knowledge of what all the variables are in any procedure, we end up guessing. The more we guess, the more the desired outcome becomes a possibility rather than a probability.

Conceptually, it is easy to envision a desired result. Our image of an outcome can be so vivid it overpowers a clear view of elements essential to the process for reaching that outcome. Focusing too much on the end result, which is only a potential truth, is often what keeps us from seeing everything necessary for the result.

Suppose you want to paint your house, but you have never painted a house before. In thinking about the project, you know you need to decide on a color. One of the first things you will do is to develop a mental image of the house painted a particular color. You know that to make it happen, you will also need to decide whether you will apply paint by brushing, rolling, or spraying and what brand of paint you will use. The first necessary steps in the process involve decisions about the specific types of materials you need:

Choice (color) → Choice (application method) →
Choice (paint brand) → Effect

You go to a hardware store, buy paint and a roller, then get home and realize you do not have a tray for the paint roller. So you revise your plan and come up with a new sequence, adding that element.

Choice (color) → Choice (application method) →
Choice (brand) Choice → (roller tray) → Effect

You go back to the hardware store (or to another store if you are embarrassed you forgot the roller tray), and maybe while you are there you add drop cloths and masking tape to the chain:

Choice (color) → Choice (application method) →
Choice (brand) Choice → (roller tray) → Choice → (drop cloths) → choice (masking tape) → Effect

In other words, by first diligently thinking the process through, you will envision otherwise hidden steps along the path to your goal, save time, and get the job done.

In everyday situations such as cooking or gardening, we may follow other people's recipes and methods that promise a successful outcome. However, human factors can interfere. Creative people may resist adhering to recipes even when they are available. If there is no set method, we may have to devise our own. The results may be brilliant or disastrous. As illustrated by many public works projects that take longer and cost more than estimated, it is difficult even for professionals to accurately envision all the requisite steps to achieve an end result.

We all have goals that involve complex chains of causation with elements we cannot possibly recognize immediately. We may not be able to see the steps that will result in finding a job after we have been laid off, or we may not be able to figure out how to make a particular person fall in love with us. There is also the element of chance, which may be downright impossible to envision. Yet many results are dependent on both careful planning *and* an element of opportunity. Suppose, in the painting example, you patronize a small hardware store with only one clerk. You arrive just after she has just dropped a gallon can of paint on her foot and closed the store so she can get medical attention.

Choice → Choice → Choice → Obstacle → No Effect

Here, you attempted to put everything in place, but when you arrived at the store there was an element beyond your direct control; chance turns out to play a role in the chain. A helpful strategy in designing any process is to assume there will be at least one unknown obstacle. Although you cannot know what the obstacle will be, you can allow extra time, money, or other resources to deal with anticipated but unknown contingencies. In this example, if all the hardware stores in your area close at 5:00 p.m. and you arrive at 4:55 to find the one you picked has closed early, it may be too late to drive to another one.

If you are painting in preparation for selling your house, perhaps you paint the exterior and all the rooms, put everything in great shape, and list your house with the most effective real estate agent in your area. Yet your house will never sell until your selling price coincides with the needs and financial resources of a buyer. As obvious as it sounds, doing everything right is not always enough. We do not live in laboratories, and some chains of causation have elements that are totally beyond our control. The element of timing is especially difficult to appreciate. We naturally want results as fast as possible. Timing can be imagined as two triangles that are rotating at different rates of speed:

At some point as they spin, the tips, or vertexes, of the triangles will match up exactly for an instant. In everyday events, the fact that we have to wait for a match is not necessarily clear. There are no spinning triangles to watch. You might be attracted to someone who happens to be in a satisfactory relationship at the moment. If you had met that person six months earlier or six months later, events might have played out very differently. When the timing is right, we tend to apply labels such as "luck" or "fate" or to declare, "It was meant to be." None of these provides an explanation of what really happened; they are a shorthand way of saying that unseen elements synchronized. Complicated situations are like playing a slot machine with thirty wheels rather than three; we do not see all the wheels. There is often no way to know about all the necessary matches to achieve a desired result. Continued experimentation, as in science, can be crucial to success. One must have the faith, motivation, and willingness to take risks until all the pieces fall into sync. Getting what we want requires not only a clear vision of chains of causation but often dogged persistence.

→ Envision chains of causation as clearly as you can from the start.
→ Make necessary substitutions or add elements to create a chain that leads to the desired result.
→ Do not give yourself false explanations when the truth is that you cannot see all the elements in the chain of causation.
→ Do not overlook the importance of patience.
→ Revise your hypothesis and have the faith to continue, even if success comes more slowly than you might like.

Being Scientific in Your Life

At the core of scientific curiosity is a conviction that greater truths exist than those presently visible to us. It would be difficult to overemphasize the usefulness of the scientific method in finding those truths. Scientific inquiry has provided peeks at how things actually work—for example, the structure of DNA, how to make vaccines that prevent diseases, and the laws of aerodynamics that allow us to design flying machines. Although science has limitations and is necessarily incomplete, it is a powerful tool of modern culture that brings us closer to objective truths.

Besides their practical application, scientific discoveries also provide emotional comfort by demonstrating that life is not quite as arbitrary as it can sometimes appear. Science does not provide us with fairness, nor does it always give us the means to control events. It does not necessarily provide answers to life's most profound questions. But by explaining processes, science holds the promise that we will increasingly be able both to understand and to affect our natural surroundings.

→ You can apply the benefits of scientific method to your own life by:

- rejecting supposedly scientific conclusions not clearly based on a rigorous application of the scientific method
- refusing to fall in love with unproven theories, even your own
- constantly developing alternative theories while trying to solve a problem
- gathering information before you attempt to resolve a dilemma, because using existing methods can save time and money
- visualizing as many elements in a chain of causation as you can right from the start, and modifying your image of the chain as you learn more
- recognizing the importance of chance, patience, and determination in achieving your desired result

7

←——————→

Media and Misinformation

On Thursday, October 15, 2009, an amateur storm-chaser's weather balloon supposedly got loose from the yard at his home in Fort Collins, Colorado. As the balloon traveled across two counties, TV, radio, Internet, and other sources reported that a six-year-old boy was feared to be aboard.[1] As the story went, he had been seen playing in the balloon's equipment compartment earlier, and he was nowhere to be found after the craft took off. Then witnesses saw something fall off the balloon in flight. For a couple of hours, the country was riveted as people stayed abreast of the latest developments and speculations. As the balloon traveled some fifty miles, no one questioned that this story deserved attention. This was breaking news.

Millions watched and waited for the story's climax and conclusion. Either the boy would be safe when the balloon touched down; or it would be discovered that he was never aboard in the first place; or, tragically, his body would be found after having fallen from the craft. Concern for the little boy kept viewers engaged as the drama unfolded.

Eventually the boy was found unharmed. He was said to have hidden in a garage attic. But when asked by a CNN reporter why he had not come out of his hiding place when people were looking for him, he looked at his father and blurted, "You guys said that we did it for the show."[2]

His response turned out to be about the only true statement of the day. The boy's father came under suspicion for staging the event to attract media attention. In November 2009, Richard Heene pled guilty to one felony count of falsely influencing a law enforcement official.[3] His wife pled guilty to filing a false report with emergency services. In other words, the event was staged with the accurate expectation that the media would not only call the episode news but give it top billing. The incident had immediacy. It involved a cute little boy. The balloon was intriguingly shaped to look like a UFO. The story promised a quick conclusion; even when it began, the end was in sight, because everyone knew the balloon had to come back down. The country was promised the opportunity to either heave a sigh of relief or grieve about a tragedy.

Staged or not, was the story ever truly news? There are plenty of six-year-old boys who are in real danger from disease, starvation, or abuse who will never receive any media attention. But we are not enthralled with stories that have vague beginnings, long middles, and no clear ends in sight. In contrast, a single incident, even if trivial or ultimately fictional, will grab attention. By the time this one was over, the only news the balloon story provided was about the media's eagerness to broadcast drama, the public's appetite for drama, and the longing of some people to be famous. The balloon-boy story helped fill twenty-four-hour news slots. Heene and the media exploited public gullibility and the belief that "breaking news" alerts are significant and warrant focused attention, which is at the core of commercially funded journalism.

Most stories of any substance began a long time ago, developed over years, and may have had dramatic moments, but are not always resolved with finality. The media cannot present neat conclusions to evolving stories, which is one reason news reporting so often drifts into speculation. Editors at mainstream newspapers, newsmagazines, television and radio stations, Internet news sources, and other outlets make daily decisions about which stories are the most salable and which ones are not important enough to deserve any column space or airtime. The winners are then placed in order of perceived importance. Television stations decide which news stories they will run first and which are alluring enough to warrant teaser headlines that require viewers to endure more commercials before the story airs. Those editorial decisions regulate the order of the information the public receives and thus its perceived significance. Implicitly, we are told what is most newsworthy, and what is not so important. We are not told anything at all about the stories that get left out. Such decisions may be shaped by presumptions about what will pique the public's curiosity, the influence advertisers exert over the media source, and editors' personal tastes. To an extent that is difficult to measure, the public defines news as whatever is presented by the news media they elect to read, watch, or listen to. Even if the stories are fully accurate, the scope of available truth is defined for the public largely by what is *made available*.

The Need for Reliable Media

The preamble to the Society of Professional Journalists' code of ethics states in part that "public enlightenment is the forerunner of justice and the foundation of democracy."[4] There is little debate that a free society calls for a free press; democracy is dependent on access to accurate information.[5] In 1967, Congress decided that publicly funded radio and television was important enough to the public interest that government support was warranted.[6]

In recent years, however, there has been concern about a general decline in journalism. At the White House Correspondents' Association Dinner in May 2009, President Obama said to the assembled journalists, "We count on you to help us make sense of a complex world and tell the stories of our lives the way they happen, and we look for you for truth."[7] At the FTC News Media Workshop on December 2, 2009, Representative. Henry A. Waxman, chairman of the House Committee on Energy and Commerce, spoke about the importance of, and threats to, quality journalism. He said, "While this has implications for media and the livelihoods of everyone associated with it, it also has implications for democracy. A free press plays an intrinsic role in getting the facts, reporting them, and making accountability possible in the public interest."[8]

Part of the problem today is that fewer journalists are doing fresh investigation, and stories are subject to greater repetition. A January 11, 2010, report from the Pew Research Center's Project for Excellence in Journalism looked at the question of where our news comes from.[9] After surveying news outlets in Baltimore, they concluded that there was no original reporting in eight out of ten stories. Rather, the majority simply repackaged previously published material. In the stories that contained original content, 95 percent came from traditional media sources, mainly newspapers and television. The Pew researchers heard little actual reporting on radio programs; it was mostly monologues and interviews with guests and callers. In both local TV and print media stories, the five most popular topics were, in descending order, crime, government, business, health and medicine, and accidents. While it can be important to maintain some general awareness of crime and even of accidents, those stories deliver little useful information. It is more important than ever to consider whether what is being presented is actually news and how important it is to our lives.

Ethical journalists endeavor to maintain standards of accuracy, fairness, thoroughness, and independence; some would add transparency to the list. Journalists are encouraged to find corroborating evidence for their sources. The Society of Professional Journalists encourages its members to seek out those accused of wrongdoing so they can respond to the charges; to identify available sources; to avoid oversimplification and stereotyping; to refrain from imposing their values on others; and to distinguish between advocacy and news reporting. Journalists are urged to be compassionate to those their story affects, show good taste, avoid conflicts of interest, and admit mistakes.[10] But as we shall see, ethical standards are not always enough.

Strategies for consumers of news include seeking out respected and objective news sources, alternating between types of media, and considering as many different sources as time and money allow. This can be as simple as alternating among TV stations every day or subscribing to a newspaper from a large city in addition to your local paper. The Internet has made it easy to consult different sources; most newspapers and television stations have Web sites. Reading about the same news events on different sites will not only tell you more about the subject matter but will give you some perspective on the sources. We grow accustomed to how a particular source reports news and may come to trust it, but obtaining news from any single source is unlikely to provide a balanced view.

TV News

A September 2009 Pew Research Center release reported that 71 percent of Americans cited television as their source of most national and international news.[11] Yet the same study reported that public perception of the accuracy of news sources in general had reached its lowest level in more than thirty years of their surveys. Only 29 percent of Americans believed news organizations were getting the facts straight; 26 percent said that news organizations were careful to avoid political bias, while 60 percent said that news organizations were politically biased.[12] Some television newsmagazines, most notably the venerable *60 Minutes*, which has been on CBS since the late 1960s, have set standards for meaningful investigative journalism and brought facts to light the public might not otherwise have learned. *60 Minutes* in particular has been extremely popular and long-lived. While its record is not perfect, the program would not have lasted so long if it had not endeavored to provide truthful reporting, if it had been too fearful of potential litigation over substantive stories, or if it had allowed itself to become significantly compromised by sponsorship concerns.

In January 2010, a poll from Public Policy Polling indicated that 49 percent of Americans trusted Fox News; 74 percent of that group identified as Republicans.[13] Dean Debnam, the president of Public Policy Polling, was quoted as remarking that a generation prior, the expectation was that Americans placed their trust in unbiased sources, but that now "they're turning more toward the outlets that tell them what they want to hear."

The popularity of Fox News may come in part from its style of presenting stories with an emotional tinge and an element of moral certainty. Unfortunately, some television news networks attract viewers by appealing to our worst traits, such as our capacity to be fearful, jealous, or angry. By stoking those emotions, networks encourage audiences to worry that they are in danger of losing what they value in their lives. Audiences are led to believe that any personal fears or doubts they have about the world are the fault of some other identifiable group of people, such as the members of another political party.

There is a significant problem with news that purports to be objective but chooses and tells stories in ways that merely satisfy viewers' predilections. The line between responsible reporting is also crossed when stories are presented more for their entertainment value than their social significance. Eager to make stories seem compelling or give the impression that they are delivering more than the continuation of an old story, television stations now caption many of their reports with terms such as "Breaking News" or "New Developments" when those characterizations are not accurate. Other contrived techniques to spice up stories include reporters asking persons on the street, "How did you feel about that?" or only slightly more subtly, "Did that surprise you?" with the hope of adding an emotional element to the facts.

Whatever TV news you watch, it is helpful to use the technique described in chapter 1 and bear in mind the agenda of the source, then examine your own reactions. Also consider:

→ Are the anchors and commentators consistently telling you what you already believe, or do they sometimes include viewpoints that genuinely make you reconsider your own?
→ Will the stories they select seem as important next week as they do today?

→ Is the news presented in a way designed simply to make you angry, or do you come away with a sense of what you might do to improve things?

Newspapers

Newspapers, heavily reliant on advertising for their revenue, face considerable financial pressures today. Average daily circulation has been declining since 1987.[14] In 2009, the *Christian Science Monitor* went from daily to weekly print production.[15] Not only has the cost of newsprint gone up, but competition with electronic media has reduced circulation. The Internet, radio, and television have upstaged the immediacy newspapers once provided. But newspapers are still widely read: the U.S. Census Bureau reported in its 2007 statistical abstract that the average adult would spend 175 hours reading newspapers that year.[16]

Back in the 1890s, melodramatic "yellow journalism" was an accepted style. Now most readers expect newspapers to provide reliable, fact-based reporting. But faced with shrinking circulations and page counts, newspapers again face temptations to sensationalize the news.

In an attempt to hold journalists accountable, the Freedom Forum First Amendment Center—Ethics in Journalism Web site posted an alphabetical list, updated April 2010, of reporters involved in plagiarism or fabrication scandals.[17] Jayson Blair is one such example. He resigned from the *New York Times* after it was discovered that he had plagiarized and concocted segments of stories written over a four-year period. In May 2005, Griego Erwin resigned from the *Sacramento Bee* newspaper when it was discovered that people she had mentioned in her columns did not exist. Al Levine of the *Atlanta Journal Constitution* was accused of taking information from Florida newspapers without crediting them. And Eric Slater, a reporter with the *Los Angeles Times*, was fired when his editors were unable to confirm details of a story on a fraternity hazing.

In January 2007, the *San Francisco Chronicle* placed on the front page a photograph of a blood-spattered doorway in Iraq along with a story about recent violence there. One elementary-school teacher wrote to the paper, saying, in part, "I need to shield my thirty 10-to-12-year old students from these horrors by dumping the unopened copies before they see them." Another reader wrote, "Have you become nothing but voyeurs of the lurid?" These sound like sincere questions about whether readers are being subjected to the effects of journalistic desperation, but they bring to light other considerations as well. Was the photograph published simply because of its graphic allure? Is a newspaper being truthful if it decides *not* to publish certain photographs that portray unpleasant realities? Should students between ten and twelve years of age be given a newspaper that omits the horrors of war? Would students' awareness of those events eventually make the world more harmonious, or would that awareness only make them callous? These questions illustrate the complexity of editorial decisions about what pieces of information are distributed. Added to the pressure from perturbed readers—obvious only because their letters were printed—the paper may also have had to field pressures from advertisers and its own staff.

Coverage of the Iraq war in particular has been a controversial and sensitive issue for both print and nonprint journalists and readers. Steve Rendall, an analyst at the media watchdog group Fairness and Accuracy in Reporting, expressed the opinion that by 2003, the public had become skeptical of war news reporting.[18] Discrepancies between preinvasion coverage and facts that later came to be known were widely noted. With some exceptions, reporters were embarrassed at having bought into the hysteria over potential weapons of mass destruction in Iraq. Judith Miller, a reporter at the *New York Times*, is one of the exceptions. In September 2002 she reported, "Iraq has stepped up its quest for nuclear weapons and has embarked on a worldwide hunt for materials to make an atomic bomb." Her source was Bush administration officials. The *New York Times* article was then used by Bush administration officials as a corroborating source to justify going to war. In other words, the source of the purported information was the Bush administration, which then used Miller's reporting to give legitimacy to its actions. When it was later determined that the information was incorrect, Miller's explanation was, "My job isn't to assess the government's information and be an independent intelligence analyst myself. My job is to tell readers of the *New York Times* what the government thought about Iraq's arsenal."[19] It would be difficult to find many journalists who agree that their job is only to parrot what they are told without making an effort to determine if it is true. Unfortunately, there are some who relate information without fully fact-checking it. Reporters can also be guilty of presenting conflicting information as simply a matter of differing opinions, even if one side's argument is clearly not based on fact, while the other's is factually accurate.

Readers often accept newspaper stories largely at face value. We could not otherwise regard them as useful sources of information. Less obviously, we accept the *selection* of articles a newspaper covers. The scope of material affects our perceptions as much as the material itself; the topics implicitly define what is important to know about.

It may seem at first glance that many stories are frivolous, but they may actually deliver important truths. A large number of newspaper stories are, for example, about people who exercised bad judgment, usually because of overwhelming emotions. The accounts can seem to be little more than voyeuristic glimpses of other people messing up. But they also serve the subtle function of providing a sense of what social rules and norms are. They can serve as a reminder about how lives can go wrong. Other stories serve as inspiration; they may describe individuals who have overcome the effects of accidents, done charitable work, or achieved business or artistic success. Without stories that tell us about other people who have failed and triumphed, we would have a far more limited sense of the dangers and opportunities in our own lives.

Unlike when we watch television or listen to radio news broadcasts, we can select the order in which we read newspaper stories, or skip them entirely. Because articles compete for our attention with other media, and with other stories in the paper, headlines are particularly susceptible to abuse. Newspapers are faced with the task of making stories appear interesting without editorializing. Sensational headlines can cause us to skip important information, or they may draw us in for no good reason.

The long-honored newspaper tradition of printing selected letters to the editor provides a valuable forum for the expression of readers' opinions. In addition to criticisms or appreciation of stories, letter writers frequently offer solutions to social and political problems, often presenting well-intentioned but unrealistic "just do this" answers to public troubles. These writers seem to miss the fact that problems persist not so much because no one else has thought of solutions, but because no one has figured out how to implement them. They remind us that ideas are deceptively easy, while their execution rarely is.

The Internet

In 1997, 18 percent of U.S. households had Internet access; by 2009, the figure was up to 68.7 percent.[20] The upward trend will likely continue. Despite this, as argued by John Nichols and Robert W. McChesney in a January 7, 2010, article in *The Nation*, it is a misconception that the Internet is to blame for the overall decline in news media reporting.[21] They believe the problems with journalism began in the 1970s due largely to media corporations' focus on profits, which trivialized journalism itself. To the extent that is true, reporters working for media corporations would have been encouraged by their employers to focus on the sensational and repeat what people already believed, rather than being provided with budgets for in-depth investigative reporting. If Nichols and McChesney are right, reporters were discouraged from presenting stories that might have been more accurate but less appealing to the public.

Has the Internet improved the availability of accurate news? Mainstream online media and ordinary bloggers attempt to capitalize on the assumption that the Internet provides not only freshly updated information but insider tips not available anywhere else.[22] Sometimes this is true; information can now be disseminated immediately by anyone and from virtually anywhere. While Internet stories can be updated frequently as facts come in, it is rare that hourly updates are important or even interesting. Between multiple online news sources and bloggers, stories are repeated, usually without new reporting but sometimes with a slant added. A report by the Pew Research Study in January 2010 referred to online reporting as an "echo chamber" and noted examples of Web sites that used the work of others without attribution as well as sites that suggested original reporting had been added to stories when none actually had been.[23]

By 2006, there were reports that YouTube's Web site was delivering 100 million videos every day.[24] By September 2010, YouTube claimed that figure had climbed to 2 billion videos a day and that people were uploading hundreds of thousands of videos daily, a rate of twenty-four hours of video every minute.[25]

In early 2007, an anonymous political video attacking Hillary Rodham Clinton was posted on the YouTube Web site. The video received more than one hundred thousand hits in two days, demonstrating the potential for an individual to reach large numbers of people through the Internet almost for free.[26] Running even a modest political ad on television would have cost tens of thousands of dollars.

But the unreliability of Internet sources is a significant problem. Nonprofessionals, whether regular bloggers or occasional posters to others' sites, are rarely as reliable as professional journalists. Nor are they accountable. In 2008, an eighteen-year old posted an Internet story claiming Apple CEO Steve Jobs had experienced a major heart attack and had been rushed to the hospital.[27] The poster claimed his source was an "insider" who asked to remain anonymous but was "quite reliable." Shares of Apple stock plunged, and the Securities and Exchange Commission began investigating almost immediately, because some traders seek to affect stock prices by spreading false rumors. In fact, Apple's stock value dropped by some $4.8 billion during the first hour of trading on the NASDAQ. After the blogger's false rumor about Jobs's health was officially denied, the stock began to recover.

One immensely popular video blogger in 2006 was lonelygirl15, supposedly a home-schooled sixteen-year-old.[28] Viewers were fascinated with her persona but also suspicious and anxious to get at the truth behind her too-polished videos. The truth eventually did emerge: lonelygirl15, also known as Bree, was actually a nineteen-year-old film student. The charade about her supposed life had been concocted by three filmmakers in their late twenties.

The current generation of Web resources, known as Web 2.0, involves social connections through which people collaborate on and share information. One of the best-known examples is Wikipedia, which invites contributions from the public on subjects of all types. Other sites allow groups of individuals to share knowledge on specialized topics with reviews, how-to tips, comments, discussions, photos, and audio and video postings.

In 2009, Shane Fitzgerald, a Dublin University student, posted on the Wikipedia page for Maurice Jarre, a French composer who had just died, a fake quotation he attributed to Jarre.[29] Fitzgerald assumed that obituary writers would be searching online for interesting biographical tidbits about Jarre. He was right. Bloggers and journalists around the world used the quotation he had posted on Wikipedia:

> One could say my life itself has been one long soundtrack. Music was my life, music brought me to life, and music is how I will be remembered long after I leave this life. When I die there will be a final waltz playing in my head, that only I can hear.

Fitzgerald believed the Wikipedia article was especially susceptible to his plant because the article did not already have any other strong quotations. As much as Fitzgerald was reviled for his deliberate deception and for taking nearly a month to confess, he proved what he suspected:

the media was generally willing to use the fake quotation at face value, even though no source was listed and even though it appeared on Wikipedia, which is not considered a reliable source by journalists or serious researchers.

Andrew Keen, author of *Cult of the Amateur*, is critical of the ability of nonprofessionals to use the Internet to share information and viewpoints.[30] It is difficult to argue against his basic premise that there is too much useless, opinionated, and incorrect material on the Internet or that much of the content does not meet standards of professional journalism. But closer to the heart of what appears to bother Keen is how the Internet has exposed the essential messiness, limitations, and narcissism of individual experience. The world no longer comes to us through a visit from Walter Cronkite's cordial persona; it is as if everyone in the world now has directions to our houses. They arrive bearing gifts that some believe resemble trash more than presents.

It is inarguable that the Internet can be and is abused. But while the Internet spreads the messy and the inaccurate along with good, accessible content, the medium gives the average person a voice. There are gems among its many bloggers and posters—people who have inside information, exclusive videos, funny thoughts, wisdom, and truths, who would never be heard from without the Internet.

→ Many schools now teach methods for evaluating the reliability of Web sites. You, too, can follow their advice to students:

- First consider the three-letter abbreviation at the end of the site's URL, or address, to determine if it is a commercial site (.com), a government site (.gov), an educational site (.edu), an organizational site (.org), or some other type.
- Check the identity of the author and his or her credentials.
- Note when the information was last updated.
- Ascertain the agenda of the site. It may be sales oriented or serve as justification for an event or idea.

- Look for clues about unreliability: errors in spelling or grammar, obvious factual errors, and strong opinions, especially those without any reference to supporting evidence.
- Consider using one of the numerous Web sites such as TruthorFiction.com or Snopes.com that research the accuracy of stories to determine whether they are true or are rumors, urban legends, or hoaxes.

YouTube, MySpace, Facebook, Twitter, and other services are changing the way we share information, and the Internet continues to be applied in new and startling ways. Google Earth took advantage of its technological capability to provide satellite images as well as ground-level photographs of carnage in Darfur showing burned villages, wounded children, and the camps of refugees; at the time, Google Earth had some 200 million users.[31] Today, law enforcement officers are forced to assume they may be on camera at any moment and that any misconduct they engage in might be displayed worldwide without even the filter of a news media organization. The Internet amplifies both the good and bad aspects of information sharing; it brings us more truth and more lies than ever before. The familiar admonition to consider the source is particularly applicable to the Internet.

Television Beyond News

More than any other single technology in the last century, television has raised awareness not only of local and world news, social struggles, and political events but also of the core of human emotions around which TV dramas are wound. Its array of programming draws from every form of entertainment. Television can create false impressions, but the extent to which viewers may cling to some of those impressions in daily life is less obvious. Television programming that relies on revenue from commercials is, in effect, the commercial for the commercials, and it needs to hold viewers' attention. The programming must also please its sponsors, so program content must entertain while avoiding controversies that could alienate mainstream audiences. Artistic and intellectual risks are not readily taken when revenue depends on mass appeal requiring easy digestion. The overall result is both glitzier and shallower than real life.

But television programming also imitates real life. Although the dilemmas characters face are unusual, they are still dilemmas viewers can imagine facing themselves. Since television's infancy, one highly popular program format has been the resolution of a complex problem within a one-hour episode. Crime shows such as *CSI*, medical shows, and dramas are compressed into that single hour or less, within which time a situation is both presented and resolved. While viewers are aware that it is only TV and that the events in the episodes skip ahead hours and days to reveal only the most interesting parts of the story, the presentations ask for our credulity. Even in science fiction programs, human characters behave in ways consistent with human nature and reflect the emotional realities of daily life. We can form likes and dislikes for characters. We feel sympathy or disdain for them and become emotionally involved with their problems, hoping for a particular outcome. The scary scenes can make us apprehensive; the funny scenes can make us laugh. That emotional involvement is not fictional but real. After watching hundreds or thousands of one-hour programs filled with action, humor, and drama, a person may develop a sense of what life might be like with no boring parts and much more excitement. With all the emotional goodies television programs offer, rather than complain that programs lack realism, viewers may regard life as somewhat disappointing in contrast. It is, of course, not the case that our lives can or should be as dramatic as those of our favorite TV characters.

TV programs can also present a distorted view of history; for example, they can make situations funny that were not remotely funny in reality. In the 1960s, *Hogan's Heroes* turned World War II into a comedy, as did *McHale's Navy*. Then beginning in 1972, the television program *M*A*S*H*, based on a novel and film, did the same thing with the

Korean War. Television programs even affect career choices; there were spikes in law school applications after the television show *L.A. Law* became popular.[32]

We watch a lot of television. The U.S. Census Bureau reported in its 2007 statistical abstract that the average adult was expected to spend a cumulative 65 twenty-four-hour days watching television that year.[33] This finding was amplified in early 2009, when the Nielsen Company reported that the average television viewer spent in excess of 151 hours each month—75.5 days a year!—watching television at home.[34]

The majority of parents are uneasy about the harmful effects of television. According to a Kaiser Family Foundation report released in 2007, 66 percent of parents favored government regulations to prohibit certain TV content in the early evening.[35] Thirty-four percent of the people responding reported being very concerned about their children being exposed to too many TV ads, and 35 percent were "somewhat" concerned. Their responses imply that they were worried television might affect their children negatively as opposed to merely wasting their time. These results suggest that television content is not something parents expect children to be able to just put out of their minds as soon as they switch it off. Excessive viewing may be especially harmful to children because they may be more susceptible to believing that what they see on TV is real. While parents are predictably bothered about portrayals of specific acts such as sex and violence, some of their concern may arise from the knowledge that television distorts reality. Television, with its highly selective presentations, is often preposterous. It *has* to be; it must make itself more alluring than the tactile world by condensing more drama, tension, humor, and glorification into its episodes than real life can usually compete with. Educational programs are the exception rather than the rule. Mislabeled "reality shows" do not depict real life but rather the discomfort of ordinary people placed in highly contrived situations. If television programs reflected the pace and content of much real life back to us, they would be tedious.

Radio

After losing ground to television, radio underwent a resurgence with the increasing popularity of talk radio. According to 2005 Arbitron data, 93.7 percent of people aged twelve years and older were listening to traditional radio each week.[36] From 2004 through 2009, one study indicated that people were still spending more than six hours a week (not online) listening to the radio.[37]

Top radio station formats include news talk/information; and country, adult contemporary, pop, classic rock, and classical music. As with commercial television, commercial radio stations make money selling advertising time; the more listeners they have, the more they can charge. The ads on any station are targeted specifically to the demographics of the station's listeners. This means the advertisements are aimed to people of a certain age group, income level, educational level, political affiliation, and degree of political activism. Advertisers also have statistics on the types of restaurants the station's listeners frequent and how often, their Internet use, their hobbies, and their informational interests.

To sell the ad time, the goal of commercial radio is to attract listeners using any lawful means imaginable. As with other forms of media, the need to continually attract an audience causes some stations to present sensational content and pander to the most easily accessible and often least honorable of our propensities. In January 2007, KDND radio in Sacramento, California, sponsored a contest on its *Morning Rave Show* in which twenty listeners came to the studio for a water-drinking competition.[38] Contestants were heckled and cajoled even as they displayed signs of illness after drinking huge amounts. One contestant described having cold sweats, while others vomited. As the program attracted listeners, it also suggested implicitly that listening to people in extreme discomfort was acceptable entertainment, and that whatever happened to the contestants was their own fault because their participation had been voluntary. Twenty-eight-year-old Jennifer Strange was one of the two finalists on the *Morning Rave Show* contest. Tragically, she died that afternoon of water intoxication, in which the normal balance of electrolytes in the body is upset by excessive water ingestion. In the aftermath, the station announced that it had fired the *Morning Rave Show* hosts who created the contest and canceled the program. In October 2009, a jury awarded Strange's family more than $16 million in a civil lawsuit.[39] If Jennifer Strange had not died, the contest would have been nothing but business as usual. The station could have gone on reinforcing the implicit notions that there is humor in suffering and that people desperate enough to compete in a stupid radio contest deserve no sympathy.

If people are listening to the radio six hours a week, radio stations have the opportunity to present meaningful, in-depth news coverage and analysis on both national and local levels. Yet only stations supported by their listeners and/or public funding have much hope of escaping compromises of journalistic and moral ethics; commercial stations have no incentive to ask their listeners to accept anything substantive. If commercial radio stations were restaurants, they would serve from the top of the old-fashioned food pyramid and offer meals made only of fats and sweets.

Some radio stations claiming to have news coverage feature disc jockeys who have skimmed the day's newspaper headlines, sometimes recite sentences from the stories, and at regular intervals demand to know, "How could anyone be so stupid?" These are not journalists but clowns reading newspapers, whose investigative journalism is limited to obtaining a copy of the paper. Sometimes they select reports of obscure events and entertain their audiences by overreacting to the stories. They may have a sidekick whose role is to laugh at the host's jokes and provide the radio version of a laugh track, occasionally adding an "Oh, my goodness." Some hosts whip up misguided anger, racism, and conspiracy fears; these tactics attract attention and raise ratings.

Radio personalities have a large megaphone they can easily abuse. On the extreme left and extreme right, they use real but abbreviated anecdotes to make their points, deliberately overlooking the fact that their examples are not necessarily representative of a trend or circumstance.

Disc jockeys fielding telephone calls from listeners can sound knowledgeable merely by controlling the topic of conversation and having a few facts in front of them that their listeners do not. They sometimes have their microphones turned up a bit louder than those of their guests or callers, and can abruptly cut callers off when the going gets rough.

While more substantive and less gimmicky, radio is not the perfect purveyor of truth either. These types of stations—to widely varying degrees—can justifiably be accused of catering to their listeners' existing beliefs, because content outside a familiar framework can alienate audiences. In addition, many of the supposed noncommercial stations now have corporate sponsors that may limit the range of stories they present. Even complete noncommercial sponsorship does not give stations absolute freedom to present cutting-edge or experimental material. While their audiences might be more open to having their horizons expanded than commercial-radio listeners, at some point they will also find unfamiliar material unpalatable, no matter how well it may reflect the truth.

Talk Shows and Commentators

Although talk shows on radio and television add to the pool of information we have available with which to form judgments, the programs vary in content, from serious discussions with well-informed professionals to tabloid entertainment. The programs often host celebrity guests and pitch softball questions that invite self-serving responses. Occasionally, a reviled guest is ambushed. While talk shows can present different viewpoints and useful facts, they are susceptible to the media weakness of honoring entertainment over all else, and they can be shallow. Commentators and guests sometimes express extreme viewpoints held by only small segments of the population. While the opinions extremists present do not represent commonly held beliefs, they draw disproportionate attention.

In May 2009, Lou Dobbs asked his CNN viewers whether they would "personally employ torture to save American lives and prevent an attack on this country."[40] Viewers responded online. Because respondents were self-selected, this was not a valid poll. The results were unscientific because they did not represent a true cross-section of the population. The results of any legitimate poll also have a great deal to do with exactly how its questions are phrased,[41] and Dobbs's question presumed that torture could *guarantee* a certain result, ignoring the fact that those employing torture have no idea if they will obtain useful information, false information to stop the pain, or no information at all. Respondents knew they would never actually be called upon to torture anyone. No matter how sincere their answers, people were aware they would never personally hear screams of pain or smell burning flesh. Dobbs had not posed a legitimate question, but he knew he could count on answers to support his arguments and help mold public opinion. Anyone calling this a poll was misusing the term. Talk shows using this sort of tactic are manipulating viewers to prop up the outrageous positions of their hosts.

Magazines

Just as with other media sources, the basic goals of popular mainstream magazines are financial: to achieve the largest possible circulation and greatest possible ad revenue. It is big business. According to Magazine Publishers of America, in 2008 the combined circulation revenue for *National Geographic* was $172.7 million; for *Better Homes and Gardens* $169.2 million; for *Cosmopolitan* $123.7 million; and for *The New Yorker* $69.8 million.[42]

To reap those rewards, magazines respond to the perpetual challenge of meeting their readers' desire for unique stories when topics have been covered again and again by the magazine and its competitors. How many times have you seen magazine covers with supposedly brand-new information about losing weight, building better abs, or conquering depression? *Cosmopolitan* magazine featured the following stories on its covers in 2008:

January: "Dirty Sexy Sex: Top Pleasure Experts Share Moves So New and Naughty, You Could Only Read Them Here."

February: "Sex Secrets: Arouse Him Like Crazy! 3 Surprising Pleasure Triggers, How to Hit *His* G-spot, Where He Hopes You'll Linger."

March: "21 Naughty Sex Tips: Tonight, Treat Him to Some Boundary-Pushing That Good Girls Only Dream Of."

April: "Be a Sex Genius! These Brilliantly Naughty Bed Tricks Will Double His Pleasure . . . *and* Yours."

May: "Our Naughtiest Sex Q&A: Yeah, We Went There!"

June: "His G-Spot: Yup, He's Got One Too, and It's Aching to Be Touched. Go Get It, Girl!"

July: "Taboo Sex: The Dirty, Sexy Moves a Man Craves in Bed."

August: "Cosmo's Big, Juicy Sex Poll: 30,570 Dudes Tell What They're *Dying* for You to Do in Bed."

September: "100 Sex Truths: Short and Sweet Answers to Burning Sex Questions. Put 'Em to Use *Tonight*."

October: "Guys Talk Sex: She Did What? Outrageous Things Chicks Do in Bed—Like the Crazy-Hot 'Fire Starter' Technique."

November: "Bad Girl Sex: 75 Tricks for Nights When You Want to Be Just a Little Naughtier."

December: "Total Body Sex: These Bed-Shaking Techniques Will Have Any Man Quivering with Pleasure from Head to Toe."

Other magazines, such as *Psychology Today*, do little more than state the obvious by illustrating the application of common sense. Others, such as travel magazines, can provide a few moments of vicarious pleasure through descriptions of visiting the islands of Estonia, hiking the Pacific Crest Trail, or lounging on the beach in Trancoso, Brazil. Articles may include some trivial adverse elements for realism, such as a problem with cell phone reception, but it would be hard to find a travel magazine article concluding that a particular trip was dull or dangerous. To sell magazines and ad space, the travel magazine must perpetually sell the overall message that travel is necessarily successful and exciting. The exotic locations pictured may look more drab and dusty when you arrive; magazines maintain readers' interest and promote their hopes by representing the truth selectively.

The ideal magazine article may best be illustrated by the *fake* magazine article. Unfettered by facts, a fake article can take dead aim at what readers want. Stephen Glass, a former reporter for *The New Republic*, is believed to have wholly or partly made up some twenty-seven articles over a three-year period, dodging publishers' fact-checkers, fooling their editors and the reading public.[43] He later said, "I loved the electricity of people liking my stories." He described a technique of fashioning stories with perhaps one fact that was true, another partially true, a third less true, and perhaps one completely untrue. Some of his articles were made up entirely. As his confession demonstrated, he was not only deceiving his readers but allowing himself to be drawn in. One example was his article "Hack Heaven," which combined all the elements of intrigue: sex, crime, cleverness, and scandal. Supposedly, a teenage hacker made his way into a company computer, revealing employees' salaries and posting pictures of naked women. The target company was said to have tried to hire the teenager, who kept raising the stakes. Glass even created a fake Web site to help support the story. Readers felt they were getting an inside scoop on a dramatic situation no one else had uncovered and felt privileged to have the source of the information.

Consumer Reports has long been regarded as an exception to the most basic conflicts of interest because it does not accept advertising. Yet magazines that do accept advertising also write product evaluations. Manufacturers routinely send their products to magazines hoping to have them reviewed, with no expectation that the products will be returned. Reviewers who are allowed to keep the products they test as partial or full compensation for their reviews are not seeing the product in quite the same way as someone who has to spend money on the item. Reviewers do not get to keep more expensive items such as automobiles, although the manufacturer will loan them the highest-priced model available. With reviews of new cars, the frequent result is a superficial, "golly-gee" article gushing about how much fun the car was to drive that says little or nothing about whether its sticker price is a bargain, or about its practicality, safety, economy, emissions, long-term prospects for reliability, or resale value.

Despite their inherent flaws and conflicts of interest, magazines, as with all media, can be useful sources of information. But magazines have had decades of practice disguising their compromises, and the ways in which they deliver less truth than their article titles suggest are not always obvious.

Photographs

A photograph can lie more quickly and convincingly than a thousand words.[44] Back in 1861, photographer William Mumler began selling "spirit photos" in which he had supposedly captured ghostlike images of the dead along with living subjects. He was accused of using double exposures to achieve the effect and was tried for fraud.[45] Mumler had many followers who wanted to believe in his abilities, and he was acquitted. There are plenty of examples of faked photographs; one of the most famous is the 1934 Wetherell Loch Ness photo, which was actually a photo of a toy submarine with the supposed neck of the monster attached to it. A still photograph made in northern California in 1977 from 16mm film purported to be of Bigfoot, but it turned out to be of a gentleman named Ray L. Wallace in a gorilla suit; Wallace's family revealed the truth after his death in 2002.[46]

Photographers have never needed digital manipulation, or even manipulation in the darkroom, to change the appearance of an image. A photographer can convey markedly different impressions merely by deciding what to frame and when to snap the shutter. With today's technology, we have far less assurance that what looks real is an accurate representation of the original subject. We are not always going to be aware of subtle alterations in photos or their effects on us. Those effects can be more serious than the residue of practical jokes; distorted images can and do affect our belief systems.

In October 2009, there were protests over digitally altered photos of female models made to look improbably thin.[47] Impressionable young women looking at the photographs in fashion magazines could come to believe that the pictures represented an ideal figure. Such beliefs can lead to anorexia or other eating disorders, with deadly consequences. Men seeing the distortions could be affected as well and conclude that women who cannot attain unrealistic thinness are flawed.

As an experiment, almost 300 people were shown photographs by researchers at the University of California at Irvine and the University of Padua in Italy.[48] Some of the pictures, of protests at Tiananmen Square and in Rome, had been changed to make the police appear more sinister. Subjects who saw the altered photos said they would be less likely to take part in future protests compared to those who saw unaltered photos. Altered photographs were enough to affect their future actions.

Whether or not a photograph is faked, visual images are especially seductive. While they take no appreciable time to comprehend, they may activate an emotional trigger. Especially today, it is critical to reject any impulse to draw conclusions based only on photographs; they are not worth a thousand words.

Books

The U.S. Census Bureau predicted that Americans would spend $55.5 billion to buy 3.17 billion copies of books of all types in 2007.[49] Nonfiction books are widely considered sources of truth; but are they? Strictly factual books strive to be, because authors and publishers want to maintain their credibility. Other nonfiction books, such as this one, may include interpretations, theories, and opinions. Facts reflected in books become outdated; a book on nutrition written in 1960 will contain significantly different information from a contemporary book.

Simply because books cite sources does not make them reliable. The sources can be poorly selected or themselves incorrect. Sometimes a book's title alone can be enough to tell you it is most likely unreliable. Any book whose title begins "Confessions of a . . . ," for example, is hoping to draw in readers with a promise of inside information. The bulk of the book may be ordinary reminiscences rather than secrets worthy of billing as "confessions."

When books do contain sensitive information, there may be efforts to limit public access to them. Concerned parents raise the most frequent public challenges, commonly in schools and libraries. The American Library Association (ALA) defines a challenge as an effort to restrict materials by removing them from a curriculum or library based on the objections of a person or group.[50] Most challenges are unsuccessful. Unsurprisingly, people are most often anxious about sexually explicit works, material thought to be socially offensive, books deemed inappropriate for certain age groups, violence, and books viewed as "antifamily" by religious groups. As the ALA points out, such challenges involve First Amendment issues regarding free speech; we cannot simply ban representations of truth that we disagree with. The ALA quotes Noam Chomsky: "If we don't believe in freedom of expression for people we despise, we don't believe in it at all."[51]

Concerns about exposing children to extreme materials are understandable. But there are those who also want to limit books available to adults. Some of the books mentioned as the most frequently challenged on the 2009 American Library Association list were *To Kill A Mockingbird*, by Harper Lee, *Catcher in the Rye*, by J. D. Salinger, and *The Color Purple*, by Alice Walker.[52] Arguably, adults are best served in their search for truth if they spend some percentage of time reading precisely the materials they are least comfortable with.

Although in the United States censorship is obviously much less prevalent than it is in countries such as China or Iran, it is instructive that even here, some people would prevent not only children but adults as well from reading certain materials. Keeping information from people is an effective way of controlling them. By limiting our reading, we keep information from ourselves.

→ Read widely.

Language and Symbols

Frank Luntz is a political consultant and pollster, best known for his work with the Republican Party to craft persuasive phrases, such as "tax relief" (meaning tax cuts) and "death tax" (meaning estate tax or inheritance tax).[53] Modifying a phrase can slyly alter perception of the concept behind it and create an implied truth. "Death tax" sounds implicitly unreasonable—now they are taxing us just for dropping dead? Yet "inheritance tax" hints at public good, a tax on the windfall from wealthy parents of an heir who may have done little or nothing to deserve the money. Despite the difference in nuance between the two phrases, they refer to the exact same tax.

During the health-care reform debate, Luntz suggested Republicans admit there was a health-care crisis but at the same time raise the specter of a government takeover of health care.[54] And in January 2010, he wrote a memo showing how financial regulatory reform could be defeated if it was cloaked in terms that related it to bailouts of the big banks—even though the specific intent of the regulatory reform was to ensure that the bailout scenario would not be repeated in the future.[55] Luntz is often referred to as a "master manipulator."

Language also conveys *unintended* meanings. Consider a typical news interview in which a man is asked about a harrowing experience, such as having a forest fire come within yards of burning down his house. The man might be quoted as saying, "You get used to living in a forested area, and you are always aware of the potential danger, but you are more frightened when a fire is headed your way." Clearly, the man is talking about himself. Yet he does not say, "I felt frightened." By using the word *you* repeatedly, he is telling us, among other things, that he is embarrassed about feeling frightened as the fire approached. He will not take ownership of his fright but uses language to suggest that *anyone* would have felt scared.

Other words carry connotations with which people do not want to be associated. For example, with the word *worry*, we predictably hear the following exchange:

"Don't worry about it."

"I'm not worried! It's just that . . ."

People do not want to be painted as worriers, so they deny being worried even if they have good reason to be. The word carries too many negative connotations for them to want to be associated with it.

People who are too timid to use the word *suspicious* use the word *interesting* in its place: "It is interesting that he did not even respond to the accusations of favoritism."

Other manners of speech are used to hide the truth or mask uncertainty. They are little more than crutches for the speaker or writer. Some of these are: "like," "basically," "if you will," "literally," "you know," "I mean." Some years ago, law enforcement came up with the handy term "person of interest" to use when officials did not want to come out and say someone was a suspect.

The world is too complex not to use some shorthand phrases in our thinking and communications. Folk sayings and proverbs provide us with quick expressions of more complex thoughts, although they are necessarily inexact. The more we rely on them to communicate, however, the more we can fall into conceptual ruts and fail to address the subject matter at hand. Some individuals seem to address every situation by applying a stock phrase, reciting lines such as "The grass is always greener . . ." or "You can lead a horse to water . . ." These are slipshod ways of thinking, because the grass does not really always seem greener, and horses can sometimes be coaxed (if not made) to drink. Nor can proverbs reflect truths if they are not wisely applied. One might observe a busy restaurant kitchen and say, "Too many cooks spoil the soup," instead of, "Many hands make light work." Without understanding the situation in that specific kitchen, it would be easy to apply a proverb and draw a mistaken conclusion.

Popular phrases such as proverbs come with a connotation of social acceptability; by uttering them, one may feel drawn a little more closely into the fabric of society. Many folk sayings have been around for generations, and others make new appearances, then live or die according to their catchiness. Advertising campaigns take advantage of our readiness to apply packaged concepts to the world. Advertisers could scarcely ask for more than thousands of people reciting phrases associated with their product, such as "Where's the beef?" "Got milk?" or "Just do it!" Advertisers also play with language to cover up negative realities; for example, a cheap camera with no focusing mechanism is called "focus free."

Punctuation can also reflect deviation from the truth. If someone is uncomfortable using a word, they may inappropriately place that word within quotation marks—called "scare quotes"—achieving nothing except to advertise their belief that it is not exactly the "right" word. It is a bit like people who turn their emergency flashers on when they drive down the freeway at forty-five miles per hour, or when they double-park. It is a signal that they know what they are doing is wrong, but they are doing it anyway.

Jokes are frequently used to convey underhanded messages. Racism, criticism, and simple meanness are packaged as humor, and objections are rebuffed with the question, "Can't you take a joke?" Often, any humor in the joke is only a sideshow, its main purpose being to convey a message that would otherwise be unacceptable.

Symbols are subject to disingenuous use as well. For years the Branded Few Motorcycle Club has used the swastika in the club's logo.[56] To most people, the symbol is permanently linked with Adolf Hitler and the Nazi Party. It is scarcely necessary to argue that the only reason a member of a motorcycle club would display the symbol today is that it is an easy way to stir up feelings of anger and dread. In 2010, the club's Web site contained a history lesson on the symbol. They discussed its use in ancient Rome, on Buddhist idols, and on Chinese coins dating to 315 BCE. They included an image of a 1907 postcard on which it was displayed as a good luck symbol. The club showed a picture of 1920s Native American beadwork bearing the swastika. All these references may have been historically accurate, but none of them did a thing to remedy the fact that any prior significance of the swastika was eclipsed when it was used by the Nazi Party in Germany. The motorcycle club knew what the swastika represents to most people today.

8

←————————→

Lies We Live With

In some areas of our lives, deception is so common we are no longer surprised by it. We expect politicians and salespeople to lie to us. We are not stunned to learn the government has wasted money or tried to cover up inefficiency. We even expect our friends to lie in some situations to spare our feelings.

Politicians

Politicians have an uncomfortable relationship with the truth. Competition for the offices they seek tempts them to promise more than they can realistically deliver, and different segments of the electorate demand satisfaction in different ways. With rare exceptions, a politician can appeal to a diverse electorate only at the expense of the truth. Honest politicians are at a severe disadvantage.

Part of the problem is that the complexity of the work done by elected officials is not necessarily obvious to those outside politics. Impediments to getting things done are not always publicized, and delays can quickly be assumed to be the result of ineptitude or corruption.

We know how the system *should* work. It should not be necessary for politicians to accept campaign donations from individuals and entities who want to buy influence. Politicians should put their personal agendas aside and always do what is best for the electorate. Voters should not be swayed by misleading attack ads. Everyone should vote in every election and do so intelligently.

Of course, that is not the real world. Backroom deals are made, and voters are influenced by unfair political attack ads. For better or worse, compromises are made routinely, for reasons obscure to most. Even though the news media have made an industry of commenting on political events, truly neutral analysis is hard to find. Television networks have their own political slants. Commentators with strong biases are pitted against one another because it is more entertaining to watch people fight than to hear rational discussions. Smaller, local political events typically receive little if any meaningful analysis through the media. Democracy at times calls on us, if we are to vote intelligently, to know more than we reasonably can. While responsible voters spend time studying the issues, nearly every voter takes some shortcuts by following intuition and general beliefs. That is where spin can take over.

The electorate, while cynical, remains tempted by campaign promises. We do not easily give up hope, whether for the specific issues we care about or for the perennial assurances of cleaner government. Campaign managers offer their candidates as blank screens, scrims of possibility on which voters are invited to project those hopes. The blank screen offered by campaigns is what is sometimes referred to as "character," a constellation of admirable personal traits that creates a safe alternative to taking positions on hard issues. Character is fuzzier than issues, but it is simpler to grasp. It is easier to pin hopes on the vagaries of character, because specific topics face equally specific obstacles. Character is about people; we all feel that we can understand people. We can thus develop an intuitive sense of whether a candidate will be aligned with our personal values when the crucial decisions are made without necessarily understanding the details of the issues themselves. Whether or not that trust in character is ultimately justified, it provides a level of comfort. Candidates try not to disabuse us of those vaguely positive associations; we know they speak in generalities and avoid giving direct answers when they can.

If Bill Clinton believed that womanizing was a privilege of the office of the presidency, he was out of touch with current standards of morality, the reach of the press, public appetite for sensational news, and the availability of DNA testing. If Clinton entertained a subjective truth about what he could get away with, it was outweighed by the public's investment in the issue of character and its desire for transparent government. His political opponents eagerly took the opportunity to fan the flames of moral outrage. An affair with an intern was a simple concept that required no special political knowledge to understand or to hold an opinion about. We all felt we understood what was involved, and Clinton's impeachment allowed us to participate in the debate from one side of the political spectrum or the other. For once, there could be no doubt to the average person that he or she understood the issue.

Clinton's actions made us question the wisdom of relying on our intuitive sense of character and the hope that some politicians, at least presidents, might be free of the deep flaws that can affect ordinary people. The sense that we could instinctively know the truth about major politicians was eroded.

Nothing in recent history illustrated the desire to believe that a president can be almost superhuman as much as the JFK assassination and its aftermath. The thick swath of conspiracy theories that continue to this day over the JFK assassination show how difficult it is to accept that *one* man with *one* gun could kill a president. It was tremendously disturbing to realize it might be that simple.

There have been other shocks to our confidence. Richard Nixon violated our trust by using illegal tactics to undermine his opponents. Nixon resigned from the presidency to avoid an impending vote for his impeachment; he was the only U.S. president ever to resign. Vice President Gerald Ford then became president and subsequently granted Nixon a full pardon. Ford's pardon, whether or not genuinely motivated by a desire to move beyond the scandal, seemed only to further damage public trust in character.

The country then elected Jimmy Carter to serve from 1977 to 1981. A Democrat from the South, Carter was likely elected because, more than anything else, he seemed to restore the country's sense of confidence in political character. Carter went on to have a troubled presidency, but aside from one or two unfortunate remarks, he unfailingly projected a down-home sense of honesty and decency.

In 1986, we learned that members of the Ronald Reagan administration had orchestrated the sale of arms to Iran to win the release of U.S. hostages. Some of the proceeds from the sales were funneled to support anticommunist fighters in Nicaragua, known as "contras"; this deal was known as the Iran-contra affair.[1] Funding the contras was in direct violation of U.S. law. Multiple members of the administration were convicted of crimes but later pardoned when George H. W. Bush became president; Bush had been the vice president during Reagan's term.

Subsequently, we were disheartened to learn that George W. Bush's promotion of the war in Iraq had much more to do with his personal agenda than with any weapons of mass destruction or supposed links between the terrorist attacks of 9/11 and Iraq. By April 2005, a Gallup poll showed that most Americans believed that Bush had deliberately misled the public.[2]

Average citizens lack the time to take tours of the political factory where the sausage is made; we would have to spend much of our free time studying politics to understand the system and each political issue that comes before us. One of the shortcuts we need is the ability to rely on character. Strategists for candidates and political initiatives accordingly dress their candidates and agendas up in the costumes they hope we will find appealing and march them past us for approval. We get spin instead of facts; we get certainty painted over uncertainty. We get the false assurances that sell more easily than truth. We are handed wars framed as patriotic acts rather than as mass slaughter. Refusals to discuss dirty government secrets are covered by the blanket of national security. Campaign slogans are used as blunt instruments to repel meaningful questions on issues. Questions about the status quo are labeled as unpatriotic. Fear of change is fueled by fictitious concepts, such as the false assertion during the health-care reform debate that "death panels" were a component of proposed health-care legislation.[3]

Distractions, such as accomplishments in space exploration, are used to help shift attention away from poverty within our own country. Ironically, the deficit has been used to distract attention from significant unemployment.

Campaigns use sneaky polling techniques to plant false ideas about the opponent by asking inflammatory questions. In the 2004 Republican presidential primary, South Carolina voters were asked if they would be more or less likely to vote for John McCain "if they knew he had fathered an illegitimate child who was black."[4] In 2008, voters were contacted and first asked if they were Jewish. If so, the caller asked questions insinuating that Barack Obama was hostile to Israel and asked if it would affect their vote if they knew that Obama was a Muslim.[5] The questions about McCain and Obama contained false suggestions about the candidates. McCain and his wife had adopted a young girl from Bangladesh. Barack Obama is a Christian, not a Muslim. Both inquiries were intended not to ask voters' opinions, but to manipulate them into spreading what they then assumed was accurate information about the candidates.

Democracy works as intended as long as our votes are based on what we believe we are voting for, rather than on a misleading slogan or inaccurate character image. It is a system that works as intended only when voters understand the issues. It does not help that our political beliefs, like our religious beliefs, are often accompanied by strong emotions that shape choices as much as our intellectual understanding of the issues. It does not help that political television commercials are so pervasive and so attuned to those emotions. We can be manipulated by politicians in the same way large corporations get away with fraud by using accounting methods so complex that few—if any—investigators can spot any wrongdoing.

A paradox of democracy is that a small percentage of the population can make a large percentage of the population believe that what is good for the elite is good for the majority. The truly rich are, for example, routinely able to convince ordinary working people that: (a) working people can legitimately consider themselves to be part of the elite class already; or (b) that working people have a significant chance of becoming part of the elite; or (c) that if they do something to harm the elite, the jobs and wages they have will be cut off, and they will have nothing. An essential message in the book *What's the Matter with Kansas?* by the journalist and historian Thomas Frank is that conservatives have been persuaded to vote against their own economic interests because wedge issues such as abortion are aligned with the positions of Republicans, and the more emotionally charged issues have taken precedence with voters.[6]

There is no simple answer to this dilemma; it is not easy to be a fully informed voter, and not everyone wants us to be. As with being informed consumers, we have to learn to ignore the commercials and the appeals to our fears, innate greed, and concerns about social status. We have to devote time to understanding the real issues and avoid the temptation to express opinions merely to give the appearance of sounding informed. We have to be honest when we do not have enough information to have an opinion. It is necessary to seek new information continually rather than mindlessly subscribe to a party line. Any intelligent person in a democracy arguably has a responsibility to look beyond the surface. Nonpartisan organizations such as the League of Women Voters make information more accessible to those of us whose lives are not steeped in political study.

Distortionists

In 2004, California governor Arnold Schwarzenegger released a premade news report to television stations regarding a plan to relax mandatory standards on worker lunch breaks.[7] What the stations received was a ready-to-air clip made to have the appearance of an actual news story. Of course, it presented a limited, skewed view, but some stations in California simply ran Schwarzenegger's piece as they received it. Others used parts of it in their reports. This was not an isolated incident but part of a growing effort to tempt media outlets with the convenience of ready-made clips at the expense of objectivity.

During the 2008 Obama–McCain presidential race, a TV ad for McCain claimed that Sarah Palin had stopped the "Bridge to Nowhere." In reality, in 2006 Palin had been for the bridge in Alaska from Ketchikan to Gravina Island, but Congress stopped funding for it, and Palin only later changed her position.[8] On the other side, a widely circulated Internet e-mail listed books Palin supposedly tried to have pulled from the Wasilla, Alaska, public library after becoming the town's mayor in 1996, but there was no evidence that Palin had ever tried to censor any specific books.[9] Some of the books on the list had, in fact, been published after she was no longer mayor.

During acrimonious debates over health-care reform in 2009, an NBC/*Wall Street Journal* poll taken in mid-August found that 45 percent of respondents believed it was likely that the government would decide when to withhold care from the elderly, while none of the proposals under consideration had suggested that possibility.[10] That fear was generated deliberately by those who stood to lose financially if significant health-care reform passed, as well as by people who felt the government would seize any opportunity to control their lives. Some rumors are spread by people paid to do so, by television and radio personalities who make their incomes by introducing sensational topics, and by the people who mistake sensationalism for the truth. The same NBC poll showed that half the people they questioned expected taxpayer money would be used to fund abortions, at a time when the House of Representatives would have allowed abortions only with the beneficiary's own money, and after Obama had clearly stated he believed the country could continue its tradition of not financing abortions as part of government-funded health care.[11]

"Spin doctors" rush to put a better face on damaging news leaks, gaffes, misjudgments, and scandals. But even the term *spin* itself is dishonest. The word evokes images of child's play: merry-go-rounds, pinwheels, Ferris wheels, and tops. "Distortion doctors" would be a more accurate label, except they are not really doctors, either; the word *distortionists* may fit them better.

Sometimes public figures appear to recognize that manipulating the facts will only damage them further and so they admit to mistakes, criticizing themselves before their opponents have the chance. More often, they hope the public will accept a quick coat of paint over the problem when they send their distortionists out to lie to us.

Through politics, power is given and taken away, and money is collected and distributed. Competing interests would like nothing better than to influence large numbers of voters with catchy slogans and misleading television commercials. But if we are willing to make the effort, we can make our representative democracy work in the way it was intended. The alternative to devoting time to understanding the political world is the risk of voting in response to false clues or refusing to vote at all, leaving control of the government to the greatest manipulators.

Friends and Strangers

Who but a true friend or a true enemy is going to tell you that you have bad breath? Your friends may be the only ones willing to tell you certain things because they care enough about you that they do not want you to get hurt out of ignorance. Your friends are invaluable for helping verify your beliefs about the world in thousands of large and small ways. Good friends can and will tell you when they disagree with your views or believe you are headed down the wrong path.

Friends will also confirm you are on the *right* path; you may discuss politics with friends over dinner, not because you are going to solve the world's problems, but in part to assure yourself that there are others who think similarly and that your own beliefs are reasonably sane. Of course, we can have too much of a good thing; the more we surround ourselves with people who agree with what we already think, the fewer new perspectives we will end up considering. Friends can also be less likely than strangers to be honest on the topics about which we are the most sensitive. Showing our friends our paintings, having them read our novel, or asking them to listen to us play the oboe may bring us nothing but ill-deserved encouragement. Our friends will sense our emotional investment and not want to disappoint or offend us. They may also be poorly equipped to offer any meaningful criticism—they may simply not know much about painting, novel writing, or oboe playing.

People with different viewpoints, and those who are not invested in maintaining a friendship with us, can be among the most helpful in identifying truths we have not considered. Consider how direct and even brutal people can be with one another in exchanges protected by the anonymity of the Internet. No doubt some of the viciousness is motivated by a need to blow off steam; the person engaging in a verbal attack may have no other outlet. But the Internet is also a place where blunt truths are expressed by people who would not dream of being so direct while facing someone in person.

Upon first meeting you, others may notice only your physical appearance and your comments on the topic of the moment. They are limited in their view of you because they do not understand your potential and may know nothing about your accomplishments. Nor will they see all your self-doubts. They offer you a limited but in some ways cleaner perspective than anyone else. Their reactions to you, whether communicated with guarded politeness or uncaring brashness, are worth your attention. You also have the chance to be someone new to them, and to yourself. You will not be burdened by mistakes you have made in the past. It is possible to be wiser or kinder or bolder with them, since they will not know about any old, contrasting behavior. What you may discover is that the updated self you present is actually the more accurate version.

Strangers have valuable truths to offer—not just in reaction to you, but in their observations about life. Everyone has unique kernels of wisdom. Our friends tend to repeat the same bits of wisdom over and over, worded a little differently each time, while strangers may offer us something new.

Yet as valuable as unfamiliar people are as sources of the truth, it can be difficult to start interactions with them. Some people—and I am one of them—are shy about initiating contact. Some of the people you approach will resist a stranger, and you may also be hesitant when someone tries to strike up a conversation. We are not always sure we *want* each other's truths. Salespeople making cold calls know this hesitation, as does a man trying to get a woman's phone number. By opening ourselves up to a stranger, we are subjecting ourselves to their versions of reality. That includes their conclusions, prejudices, assumptions, opinions, and characterizations. Inevitably, the other person will make some effort to convince you those perceptions are valid. He or she may indirectly ask you to appreciate how clever and special he or she is. It can be tiring to sort out a constant stream of unfamiliar viewpoints. People who push their own versions of reality especially hard can leave you craving some solitude so you can get back to your own thoughts and feelings.

Interactions among groups of people, as in meetings, theoretically provide an opportunity to exchange diverse experiences and wisdom. Such exchanges happen when there is genuine communication and truths are shared. Group dynamics, however, can pose obstacles to the exchange of meaningful information. In many groups, the verbal exchanges are chaotic, with people far more interested in speaking than listening. Hierarchy can restrict input so it comes only from certain people. Discussions are best facilitated if order is imposed and everyone with something to say is actually listened to.

In some group situations, such as when a group of coworkers goes to lunch, the focus may not be on the discovery of one another's differences as much as it is on conformity. Certain topics—work, sports, celebrities, electronic gadgets, office gossip—may be acceptable for conversation. Anyone who deviates far from the group norm by attempting to introduce a more personal or controversial subject, or just a new topic, may encounter resistance. That resistance may be expressed as polite disinterest, teasing, mockery, or outright hostility. Divergence can also be controlled through ridicule of a person's dress, hobbies, or opinions. Yet if no individual is allowed to expand the group consciousness by expressing differences, by sounding or even looking different from the rest, the pool of shared information is likely to be shallow. The truths each individual might have offered to the group will be lost.

Marlon Brando once said that everyone is an actor. We pretend to be interested when we are not, pretend to like gifts we are not thrilled with, pretend to like people when we want things from them. We say we understand and agree with ways of thinking in order to fit in, or we say we do not understand, also to fit in. Even relationships that are mainly genuine contain some artificial elements. We hold some things back that might hurt or offend our friends or claim to feel differently about certain subjects. It is an illusion to insist that any of our relationships are one hundred percent truthful; that is just not human nature.

We can surround ourselves with people who tend to agree with us or with people who will provide constructive criticism and challenge us to do better. Choosing who is around us will have a significant effect on our thought processes, actions, and self-image. People can bring us both truths and illusions.

→ Think carefully about the effects other people have on you . If you have any choice, put yourself in the company of people who will help you see the truth.

Stereotypes

If someone is raised believing that certain people have particular traits and has no experiences to counter those beliefs, the beliefs may go unquestioned. Unfortunately, stereotyped groups are usually identifiable by superficial indicators such as gender, race, or other physical characteristics. It is thus possible to acquire and maintain pseudoknowledge about groups without actually interacting with them. If we are forced to communicate with people in order to assign them to a group not based on physical appearance, it is harder to stereotype them.

Women are _____.
People from India usually _____.
People from Mexico tend to be _____.
Elderly people are mostly _____.

As you read the above, did any words come to mind? Did you catch yourself censoring any? People do form impressions of identifiable groups; sometimes the impressions are true as generalities, but they are not applicable to each individual member of the group. Stereotypes are reinforced among our immediate social contacts, in movies, and on television programs. Every time a writer, director, or producer presents a fictional character that does not fit within a range of behaviors commonly associated with an ethnic, gender, or other identifiable group, she risks calling attention to the fact that the production is a fiction. That attention can distract from the story, and most often the choice about how to portray characters will be one that panders to expectations. There may sometimes be truth in generalities, but they are large obstacles to recognizing what is unique about each of us.

Fads and Fashions

A fad is an item that is hugely popular for a short time and then disappears from our culture about as quickly as it appeared. Hula hoops were a great example of a fad.[12] Marketers have successfully used the fad effect to sell products. For example, low-fat foods were popular for a while, then low-carbohydrate foods were fashionable. We had the Atkins Diet, the cabbage soup diet, the South Beach Diet, the Drinking Man's Diet, the grapefruit diet, and many others. Once large numbers of people are doing something, it can seem there must be a good reason.

But taking cues from what other people are doing can be misleading. We can pay more attention to what we believe we *should* be experiencing than to what our own senses tell us. In blind taste tests, a study at the California Institute of Technology examined whether the people who believed they were drinking expensive wines rated them higher than less-expensive products.[13] Magnetic resonance imaging used in the tests showed that the part of the brain that reacts to pleasant experiences lit up when subjects believed they were drinking wines in higher price ranges, even when significantly cheaper wines were substituted. In one blind test, tasters selected a five-dollar wine as the best of the lot, even against much more expensive wines.

Clothing manufacturers, designers, wholesalers, retailers, advertisers, and others involved in chains of clothing distribution make money when the public is persuaded that a style of clothing, even though still serviceable in every other respect, can no longer be worn because it is out of fashion. The way to achieve that result is, of course, to introduce a new fashion. The old fashions go to secondhand stores as soon as wearing them would diminish a person's social status and power. Younger people, having had less time to discover and become comfortable with themselves, are particularly susceptible to the pressure to be fashionable. They may view older, unfashionable people as being out of touch without realizing that older people may have actually outgrown the need to be fashionable.

Other perceptions of the truth are influenced by innumerable assessments about the validity of what others are doing. The speed of any given car on a highway in the United States is determined less by posted limits than by how fast everyone else is going. The unlucky speeder who is ticketed is apt to say she was only "going with the flow of traffic" and may honestly feel her citation is unfair for that reason. At busy city intersections, groups of people will wait for the pedestrian signal, but if one person starts to cross against the light, others frequently follow. We have rational rules that are supposed to define how things work, but we often pay more attention to the realities of what others do.

CHAPTER 8

Finance

A former national television financial commentator told me that in May 2008, he had publicly predicted an economic downturn. Although he did a tremendous service for the viewers who followed his advice, he made some colleagues unhappy back at the brokerage firm where he also worked. He was pressured by the firm to quit television because brokers had started losing commissions as concerned investors pulled away from the stock market.[14] As we all know, the economic downturn that followed was disastrous. The television station and the public lost a perceptive commentator because he spoke honestly, and some brokers were more interested in short-term personal gain than in delivering sound financial advice.

That was the essence of the problem; most people did not want to step back and see it coming. Inflation had been tamed and the economy had generally been strong since 1983. Stock prices went up; home values skyrocketed. The system appeared sound, and there was no end in sight. No one was inclined to question a good thing. Investors and lenders began taking greater risks in the face of continued prosperity. Subprime loans proliferated based on the expectation that housing prices would continue to rise. Too few were willing to look at the truth of the big picture. Economists and ordinary people knew housing prices and stock values could not keep rising forever, but everyone wanted the prosperity to last just a little longer.

The stock market is notoriously subject to irrational decisions, with buy and sell orders based on impressions rooted in fear, greed, or scanty pieces of information.[15] Psychologist Paul Andreassen conducted an experiment in which he determined that investors who paid attention to nothing but the performance of a stock portfolio made better decisions than people who were given bulletins of information about the companies whose stocks they held.[16] At least in this experiment, one group of investors was paying attention to the wrong clues. Terry Odean at the University of California, Berkeley, observed that investors tend to develop a false sense of confidence when they have information.[17] Investors frequently place too much value on information simply because it is new, not because it is correct.

Most of our personal transactions are not with investments but simply with buying things in a world where it is important to think twice about supposedly good deals. For example, a computer printer may be inexpensive or even come "free" with another purchase, while its ink cartridges, which cost $100 each, over the next several years will set you back hundreds if not thousands of dollars.[18] It is the same with replacement parts for many products.

Credit cards cause tremendous problems for some. We all understand very well that after handing over a piece of plastic, a bill is going to arrive. Still, there is the strange experience of obtaining something for nothing when buying on credit. The time lag between obtaining the good or service and the arrival of the bill creates a disconnect. Credit cards provide an illusion of wealth, granting buying power well beyond available cash. Credit card companies enjoy great financial return when consumers charge more than they can pay off each month. Buying power can quickly become an expensive illusion to maintain.

Consumer Rating Inflation

Consumer ratings are easy to find on the Internet, and valid reviews can be extremely useful. The most obvious potential problem is the false review, a positive statement planted by a marketer, and/or a negative review planted about a competitor. Two such documented instances involved DeLonghi and Belkin products, for which positive reviews had been written not by customers but by employees.[19] Less obvious is overrating by genuine consumers; once a person invests money in a product and spends time using it, there is a tendency to want to justify the investment as a smart decision. If you look at commercial Web sites with five-star (or similar) rating systems, you will see that many consumer ratings are five stars. Some ratings are no doubt fake, but if three stars is supposed to mean just so-so, most products are rated higher than that. How many other similar products has the reviewer actually tried out? Where are the truly bad products? When we purchase an item, it becomes an extension of ourselves, a reflection of our good taste. We dislike being associated with anything that has a negative taint. Even people who post negative reviews frequently begin by explaining how they were misled into making the purchase. Just about no one admits to exercising bad judgment.

Business

Many of the restrictions we take for granted today that prohibit child labor, limit emissions of air and water pollutants, or bar false advertising came into existence only after disputes over facts and the interpretations of facts. Child labor was cheap; it is less costly to pollute than to restrict pollutants; there is money to be made by duping people. Today there are other debates, including those over what employee benefits should be mandated, limits on greenhouse-gas emissions, whether we should be obliged to recycle old materials, what constitutes an antitrust violation, and which business activities should be taxed. Because the fundamental goal of a business is to make money, anything that gets in the way is its potential enemy. In these debates, truth is frequently in the way.

There will always be conflict over the extent to which businesses should be regulated. All the arguments come down to a more basic question: at what point should the abilities of a business to acquire wealth be restricted in order to promote the common good? To the business, the capacity to make money is perceived as a right rather than a privilege. The business may point out that it provides jobs in the community, delivers useful products, and pays business taxes that are used to benefit the public. Yet many community members believe that it is closer regulation that promotes the common good.

An objective analysis might indicate that taking away the incentive of capitalism—the ability to acquire individual wealth—may cause the people who create and operate businesses to lose their motivation. The business might be reminded that its enterprise does not exist in a vacuum but within the protections and opportunities society offers it. Yet both sides are likely to present their positions as the only relevant truths.

Most people live with more compromises to truth in a business context than they might like. Few individuals can exist in a business organization for long by speaking the truth about the organization's weaknesses, or even by failing to place undue emphasis on its strengths. A server in a restaurant will be fired for telling customers that some of the dishes on the menu are awful, and real estate agents will have a hard time making a living if they advise young couples that the house they love is beyond their budget. No one gets along in the world for long by voicing every single truth they perceive.

Yet according to Samuel Culbert at UCLA's Anderson School of Business, when people are more honest in work settings, the companies they work for actually do better.[20] Open exchanges promote constructive change, and the best, most accurate ideas usually win out. By contrast, in a company culture that encourages deception, people come to realize they are regularly being deceived, and they become demoralized. Unfortunately, internal company honesty is not the prevailing model. Speaking the truth is more often a liability for the individual in a business environment in which honesty is not genuinely encouraged.

Businesses facing competition may engage in practices that would bother consumers who knew all the facts. One example is the rebate. A retailer can boldly advertise a low price "after rebate," which places the burden on the consumer to collect. The seller obtains the full price at the time of sale, while the consumer has to go through a sometimes cumbersome process to get the refund from the manufacturer. The effect is an interest-free loan to the company that made the product. Holding

10,000 rebate credits of $100 each gives the company $1 million to play with in the short term.

According to Missouri Attorney General Chris Koster, there are few federal or state laws regulating rebates, and less than 40 percent of mail-in rebates are ever claimed. (Other estimates vary wildly, from 1 to 80 percent).[21] In a Canadian Broadcasting Company interview, Sridhar Moorthy, a marketing professor at the University of Toronto, recited redemption rates of 2 to 50 percent.[22] Most of the complaints the Missouri attorney general's office receives involve extensive delays in payment, nonpayment, and remuneration in a form other than a check, such as a gift card. One estimate is that unclaimed rebates are a $2 billion annual windfall to retailers and their suppliers.[23]

In a March 2004 article in *Network World*, James E. Gaskin claimed manufacturers had resisted electronic rebates because of fear there would be higher claim rates. He also wrote that customers who redeemed product rebates ended up spending three times as much money as those who did not.[24] He explained that the paperwork for rebates is often shipped overseas, creating delays and errors—which, ironically, the overseas companies typically charge manufacturers fees to straighten out.

Companies game the rebate process in other ways. There is always a deadline, and people miss deadlines. Even more insidiously, the advertised rebate is sometimes not cash but a gift card that can be used only to purchase more products from the same seller. Because gift cards are not reliably redeemed either, the seller then gets a second shot at keeping the customer's money.[25] It is difficult to imagine that many customers are buying products that offer rebates while making the deliberate decision not to bother obtaining the rebate. Even if we accept a relatively generous estimate of a 50 percent rebate claim rate, it means half of us are kidding ourselves and essentially using the rebate offer as an excuse to go ahead and buy what we want.

In part, the problem of the rebate and other successful petty marketing deceptions is created by how we associate wealth with cleverness.

The people who invented rebates and cheap printers with expensive ink cartridges are not identified as public enemies whose pictures are displayed in post offices or shown on *America's Most Wanted*. Instead, they are probably admired by their neighbors for the expensive cars they drive and exotic places they vacation. We tend not to question success.

9

⟵——————⟶

Advertising: Do You Believe in Magic?

Ads stimulate desire. They speak to our existing wants and secret discontents. Advertisers bring the discipline of science and the emotional effect of art to bear on potential consumers. Studies, tests, and focus groups determine which presentations will sell more products and identify those that will not. If ads convey any useful information, it is only incidental to the goal of creating desire.

A Short History of Advertising

An ultimately successful ad may be initially hard for even its creators to recognize. Different ads speak to different types of consumers, and advertising theories differ. Yet some of its models have existed for decades. They include the Starch model developed in the 1920s—an ad must be seen, read, believed, remembered, and acted upon[1]—and the DAGMAR (Defining Advertising Goals for Measured Advertising Results) model,[2] which calls for:

- making consumers aware of an item
- describing what it is
- communicating what it will do for the consumer
- creating a conviction to buy it
- inspiring the motivation to take action on that conviction

Many other traditional advertising rules are outdated, such as those advocated by advertising giant David Ogilvy, including "Give the facts" and "Don't be a copycat."[3] Ads now provide little factual information about products and instead attempt to create moods, concentrating on subjective rather than objective truth. Advertisers can skip steps, aim for our emotions, and get to the punch line more quickly when ads use consumers' existing factual knowledge. A car ad does not need to waste time telling us what a car is. Instead, it will focus on promoting the illusion that ownership of the car will lead to a new and better lifestyle. An hour in front of a television set will confirm that ads do copy one another in form and style. Once a style is established, ad agencies and their clients may be afraid to try anything that does not look like the other ads they are accustomed to seeing.

Depending on whose estimates you accept, the average person is subjected to between 250 and 3,000 commercial messages every single day. Despite the saturation and despite our awareness that ads try to manipulate perceptions, they work. Just how manipulative is advertising? Can ads sell us things even when we know the advertisers' claims are exaggerated at best and false at worst? Can crafty ads make us do things we do not really want to do?

Not in the way you may think. Subliminal advertising was thought to have widespread, insidious effects amounting to mind control. However, Anthony Pratkanis and Elliot Aaronson were unable to find any documentation of such effects in their review of literature on subliminal advertising collected over a period of several years.[4]

Suspicion about the effects of advertising is easily fueled. The most famous subliminal advertising claim was that of James Vicary, a theater owner in the 1950s who announced that he had dramatically increased his popcorn and Coca-Cola sales by flashing split-second images of messages on a screen, too quickly to be consciously detected. It subsequently became clear that Vicary had misrepresented his results.[5] Yet for years, the public seemed willing, almost eager, to believe that this level of manipulation of consumers was possible. Part of the reason must have been no more complicated than that people had no information to the contrary. Doing experiments to measure the effects of subliminal messages involves spending time and money. There was no Internet. If information was available at all, it was through research at a library. Without ready access to information, we may suspect the worst. People were ready to believe their perceptions were being toyed with in ways they could not even detect, perhaps in part because they already felt toyed with. The belief about the effects of Vicary's experiment persisted; in 1972, Beatrice Trum Hunter reported in *Consumer Beware* that Vicary's Coca-Cola sales went up 18 percent and his popcorn sales went up 57 per cent.[6] At the time of this writing, reports that Vicary's claim was true are still being circulated via the Internet.

Exploiting Our Weaknesses

What was behind the public willingness to believe Vicary's claim? Despite the Pratkanis and Aaronson study and the fact that Vicary was compelled to back off his initial claims, we know that advertisers and others do try very hard to manipulate us. Even if subliminal advertising is entirely ineffectual, we are still subjected to ads aimed at our emotions rather than our rational minds. Ads sneak into our consciousness even if we think we are immune to their influence. As advertisers have long known, we do not always use reason or complete information to make decisions. Knowing that advertisers are tapping into the least rational parts of ourselves, we are suspicious not only about the deviousness of the ads, but about how easily we might be led to respond to them.

One tactic ads use is to appeal to our desire to conform. People conform most when they are insecure and emotionally motivated.[7] A teenager may feel intense pressure to wear what he perceives to be the right brand of jeans or sneakers. Recently arrived immigrants may go out of their way to display their patriotism. An uneducated person may strive to use complex words in front of more educated people, and some self-conscious tourists take great pains to blend in with the natives. If owning something can make an insecure person feel like an insider, they are more likely to buy it.

Advertisers also use cognitive dissonance, a technique that makes use of the uneasiness that arises when people are presented with pieces of related but conflicting information.[8] When people are told about something that does not fit comfortably within their existing belief system, they may dismiss it as untrue or distort it so that it fits. Or they may accept it as true, then look for a way to change it. As pointed out in *Twenty Ads That Shook the World: The Century's Most Groundbreaking Advertising and How It Changed Us All,* advertising can convince us that a problem exists, then offer to sell a solution.[9] Certainly the more an ad convinces us something is wrong with the way we are in the world, the more compelling it can be. If you can be made to believe, for example, that people will look down on you unless you drive a new car, you may be persuaded to go into debt to buy a car you cannot really afford. But while advertising seeks to shake us up, it also has to reassure us that we will not have second thoughts about being persuaded. Intriguingly, people more frequently review the ads of brands they have already purchased, as opposed to ads for other brands or products.[10] This implies that one component of an effective advertisement is its assurance to prospective purchasers that even *after* the purchase, convincing ads will still be around to reassure them they did the right thing. Consumers want to know they will be able to respect themselves in the morning.

These findings are all significant not only to advertising but to the general proposition that we tend to accept a new fact most readily if it:

- provides a method for resolving cognitive dissonance
- is communicated in an appealing way

- is seen as meaningful or compelling
- comes with a promise of continued assurance it was the right choice

Studies of advertising suggest we shut out or discount new perceptions that are not compelling, even if they happen to be true. Shutting new things out is a natural defense mechanism to reduce the distraction of meaningless stimuli. Advertising's task is to overcome this resistance. Ads can be compelling if they engage us by making us *feel* something, so the advertiser typically appeals to our emotions far more than to our reasoning ability.

Internet and Infomercials

Internet advertising tends to be strident. It has to make things look good very quickly. Internet marketers are becoming increasingly sophisticated at tracking what shoppers look at and purchase from Web sites, allowing the marketers to offer targeted ads to tempt a particular shopper. As a result of their aggressiveness, Internet ads expose the dynamics of advertising with more transparency than conventional ads.

The ceaseless stream of spam e-mails we receive suggests that there is a vast horde of people eager to take advantage of us. What spam e-mails offer is typically too good to be true. Yet if a larger percentage of the population did not bite—if fewer people invested in what sounded too good to be true—the quantity of spam would be significantly reduced. Spam e-mail may look ridiculous to most, but the e-mails are not much more than mainstream ads taken to an extreme. These transparent come-ons show how willing we can be to let wishful thinking take over.

Nearly as transparent, television infomercials are repetitive and typically unsophisticated. Many play on our strong desires for easy solutions to chronic problems. Infomercials rely heavily on actors with hyperenthusiastic voices; the dialogue has a forced, unnatural quality and makes liberal use of the words *great, really,* and *fantastic.* The actors generally do a poor job of faking enthusiasm.

Infomercials emphasize how easy the product is to use and how quickly results will appear. Typically, they feature an audience of at least one observer who pretends to be mesmerized as she watches the product in action. The basic messages are always the same: *What we are offering will make change easy and painless. Your life will be better.* Already wanting to believe these things, some viewers take the plunge and order the product. A visit to any thrift store confirms the aftermath. There is no gorgeous, smiling model to display the exercise equipment, describe how much fun it is to use, or marvel at how quickly fat will melt away. In the thrift store, exercise equipment, kitchen gadgets, and other items originally sold on television still look new, just a little dusty. They are the residue of successfully marketed illusions.

Operators Are Standing By

A late-night infomercial for a small blender aired for years. The device appeared to do no more than the standard kitchen blender most people already own, but it was advertised with great enthusiasm as being able to do "any job in ten seconds or less." It could make salsa in three to six seconds and sorbet in eight seconds and could blend muffin batter equally quickly. Distinguished from larger blenders by its tiny capacity, this blender did not have to run very long to mash the handful of ingredients it could hold. No doubt the blender could do "any job in ten seconds or less," on a small scale.

But the advertisers did not stop there. By claiming that the blender could "do any job" in those ten seconds or less, the infomercial implied that all that mattered was the time the blender was running. Of course, the time a blender motor is turning is only a fraction of the overall preparation time for most dishes. The salsa took little more than six seconds to blend, but on television, the ingredients were already lined up on a cutting board, ready to go. The vegetables were washed. The garlic and onions were peeled. To distract from the reality that some dishes also required post-blender cooking, actors chatted and started other jobs while a microwave did its work.

This infomercial pushed the implied truth that viewers could complete the *entire job* in ten seconds—preparation, blending, and cooking. The presentation orchestrated events like a magic show, with audience attention distracted at critical moments and always funneled toward the conclusion that the blender could do anything in ten seconds. Everything that came before and after the ten seconds of blender operation was minimized. Anyone who wanted to believe the blender could turn her into a master chef in ten seconds and save her from the hassle of preparing meals was encouraged to think just that. All that was necessary was to pay attention to the wrong cue—that the tiny blender could turn its payload to mush in ten seconds or less.

Drinking Buddies

Most forms of advertising have far less time than infomercials to encourage magical thinking. Ads may be compressed into thirty-second television commercials or placed on billboards or in magazines or newspapers, where they must work almost instantly. Billboards, virtually the opposite of the drawn-out infomercial, can sell perceptions just as effectively if they are well designed. A few years ago in San Francisco, a billboard was prominently displayed where thousands of motorists could see it every day while traveling south on Highway 80. It featured a photograph of several attractive women who either were, or were meant to look, Russian. The women were looking at the camera with apparent interest. The only words in the ad were "Stolichnaya Vodka." The ad offered no information about how the vodka was made, why it was superior to other vodkas, or why anyone should even drink vodka. Its message might have been baffling except for the fact that the billboard itself was only one of three components that made it work. The other two were:

- the preexisting knowledge of the people seeing it
- the willingness of those viewers to combine their preexisting knowledge with the images on the billboard to create a fantasy, consciously or unconsciously, as they continued down the freeway

The advertisers were confident that motorists already knew Stolichnaya was a Russian vodka; they did not distract from their message by stating the obvious. The advertisers may have also relied on a vague public awareness of a flourishing Russian mail-order-bride business, which some see as only one or two rungs up the moral ladder from prostitution. By relying on one or more connotations, the ad could work in seconds. Viewers—not the ad itself—supplied most of the message. With these components working together, it activated fantasies. The first was that *the women looking coyly at the camera are easily available.* Like the vodka, they could be purchased. Another connotation was, *Drink this vodka and these women will be yours.* (A third connotation may have been, *Or at least then you won't care as much that they're not yours.*)

Each message was based on what men already know all too well. Men know they are still the ones who are traditionally expected to ask women for a date or for a dance. They are usually the ones who have to try out opening lines and field rejections. Men know it is easier to do this when they have had a drink. All the billboard needed to do was provide a reminder that alcohol helps and associate that help with a particular source of alcohol. The billboard's ultimate message was that this vodka could fix a man's love life. Specifically, whether viewers ended up with a beautiful Russian woman, some less-desirable woman, or no woman at all would not matter as much after a few belts.

You Are Special

With the economy still looking good at the end of 2004, there was a rash of television commercials with the common theme of surprise gifts of luxury items. In one, a man carried a very small box. When he handed it to a woman, before she even opened it, she kissed the man and almost jumped on him with excitement. A similar ad showed a man ushering a woman out to the driveway of a suburban home to show her a new Jaguar, which generated a similarly enthusiastic emotional response. The most blatant message? Buy her this luxury, get sex. This type of ad reinforces old stereotypes that men are the financial providers and women are the grateful recipients of the fancy items their men wish to bestow.

Anyone in the role of provider, whether male or female, wants to feel successful in that role, especially because it requires sacrifices. Being a provider means being dependable and unexciting. It means buying a station wagon instead of a sports car. It means going to work every day and getting worn out pleasing others. It means putting many of one's own desires on hold and not running up credit card bills on electronics, fancy dinners, entertainment, or exotic trips that do not fit into the household budget. Providers may go off every morning to jobs they do not love. They go on days when they are not feeling well, on days when they know there will be problems to deal with, on days when they are afraid of being fired, and on days when they would rather quit and go home. They may return from work frustrated and feeling belittled but too proud or too concerned about being perceived as whiners to say anything. These providers would love to, at minimum, feel appreciated by their families.

Yet their very dependability makes their efforts so routine that they are not regarded as doing anything extraordinary. They are not likely to hear their spouse say, "Thank you for going to work every day." If their dependability is not actually taken for granted, it may still seem that it is. Ads for luxury goods show us a provider who has transformed the fruits of dreary toil into something tangible, luxurious, and dramatic, for which he receives the enthusiastic appreciation he wants.

Luxury items are just plain more exciting than groceries, utility bills, or mortgage payments. A luxury gift serves as a lens, focusing months or years of energy into the single, sparkling moment of its delivery. It is special. It commands attention. The expressions of intense appreciation on the faces of the recipients in these advertisements are undeniable. As with the vodka billboard, these luxury-item television commercials say nothing about the virtues of the gifts. Instead, they are all about the feelings the items can evoke.

Whether purchasing an expensive gift will satisfy the need to feel successful and appreciated, and for how long, are legitimate but often academic questions. The job of the ad is to cause a sale. With luxury goods it may not matter much what happens after the money is spent. An ordinary hard-working person who spends a substantial amount of money on something he does not need is not likely to be a repeat customer anytime soon.

If an ad is for something more practical, such as a juicing machine, the image displayed will probably be of a glistening glass of fresh juice being raised to the lips of a satisfied, healthy owner. We will not see the owner scrubbing out the machine. We are invited to forget what it will take to get it fixed when it breaks down. We are invited to believe only that it will make our lives wonderful; we are encouraged to pay attention only to those clues that will make us buy the product. If ads present the truth, it is highly selective truth.

While ads are dishonest in the way they emphasize only particular truths and in the way they cheerfully encourage fantasy, they also reflect deep truths about our fears and desires. Advertisers reach as deeply into the core of human experience as they can to increase their market share, affect as many people as possible, and not allow individual personalities to interfere. To borrow a phrase attributed to psychiatrist Clotaire Rapaille, ads often appeal to our "reptilian hot buttons."[11] Triggering our most basic feelings can be counted on to elicit a reaction in all but the most extraordinary people.

This includes tapping into:

- our fears and discomforts
- our desire to be happier
- our appetite for sex
- our wish for social status

Most of our hot buttons need little discussion. Although status may seem to be a less-basic concern than the desires for food and sex, it is also a crucial advertising tool. Our image of our place in the world distances us from the rougher existence we know could be ours with just a few turns of bad luck. With a lost job, divorce, injury, or serious illness, all but the very fortunate among us can be in deep financial trouble within months. We have seen homeless people. We know there is routine starvation in parts of the world, and we know those affected are human beings, just like us. So we assure ourselves that these people are *not* just like us. To prove this to ourselves, we need evidence. Some evidence is both readily available and rational: a job, a working spouse, insurance for the unexpected, and savings to fall back on. But we may exaggerate in our minds just how long we could maintain our lifestyle without an income. We may refuse to think about it and comfort ourselves with things that can be seen and touched: the house or apartment we live in, new clothes, electronic gadgets, a fancy car, an expensive watch or jewelry. Yet a Rolex tells time no differently than a more modest watch, and the most luxurious cars still serve the essential function of taking us from one place to another. Advertisers constantly urge us to forget that function is more important than status, and we may buy expensive things mainly as proof that we are *able* to buy them. Consciously, we tell ourselves we buy nice things because we appreciate or deserve them. That may be, but the more possessions and status symbols we have, the more we feel insulated from hardship. And if we have the best, we must *be* the best.

Advertisers sell people things they do not need or are barely able to afford even as their ads create desires beyond all reason. Advertising works by touching our fantasies and fears. Ads give life to feelings on the edge of conscious awareness. It makes those feelings seem a little more real, and then it offers ways to address them. Ads tell us we can be happier, wiser, thinner, more enlightened, more popular, more successful, and more secure—if we just believe in the magical worlds on television screens and billboards, in magazine and newspaper ads. In those worlds, people smile as they exercise, cook anything in ten seconds, possess a bevy of Russian women, and receive the appreciation they deserve.

10

←——————→

Fooling Ourselves

I was tempted to leave this chapter out. Some people who read early drafts did not like its suggestion that we sometimes see the world only as we want to. But turning away from truth and refusing to deal with unpleasant realities can be at the core of private as well as global conflicts and is thus too important to ignore.

We Do Not Always Want the Truth

We have to deal with the truths we do not like if we want to live an authentic life. But we would rather believe we are likable than accept that sometimes we are difficult to deal with. We prefer to imagine that we can and should have all the material comforts we desire, rather than acknowledge that our finances are limited. We pretend that it does not matter if we indulge in that extra piece of cheesecake, rather than take responsibility for decisions that affect our health. Life presents a steady stream of choices as to what to believe, and it is easier to accept statements such as, "You'll live to be a hundred," "You always do a great job," and "You're a fantastic lover" than their opposites.

We choose which concepts we believe are valid, and we are biased in our own favor when making those judgments. That bias interferes with our ability to live in a genuine way.

We are further limited if we avoid testing beliefs once we adopt them. At the most extreme, we even seek out false information to support what we want to believe by inviting others to lie to us:

"Does this dress make me look fat?"

"Did I wake you up?"

"Did you enjoy my fruitcake?"

To perpetuate beliefs we like, we also try to trick others into believing the same things we want to believe. We may floss frequently only during the week before a dental checkup, or start eating better only in anticipation of the lab work that precedes an annual physical. It is as though by duping the medical professional, we can avoid embarrassment and validate self-deception. All we have done is reinforce false perceptions, inviting decay and disease in the process. Enforcing some discipline on ourselves and making preventive measures a permanent part of our lifestyle would entail recognizing and accepting that each of us is responsible for the choices we make on a daily basis. But often we would rather fool the people who would steer us back toward reality.

We give ourselves false explanations to avoid facing risk. A woman may want a more satisfying relationship, one in which she feels loved and understood. If she is afraid to start looking, she may tell herself, "All the good ones are taken," then mentally list all the unavailable men she knows. Or perhaps the same woman wants a more challenging, lucrative career. She may put obstacles in her own way by saying to herself, "The economy is so terrible that nobody is hiring." In reality, if she were willing to risk disappointment, she might be perfectly capable of finding a more satisfying relationship and a better job.

There are constant temptations to turn away from the truth. Just as it is uncomfortable to take risks, it is also uncomfortable to see what we should be doing and to be aware that we are afraid to go ahead and do it. Ignoring the truth can be an expensive choice because the truth can help us avoid problems, and ignorance can cause us to miss experiences we could otherwise have. We can hide from the truth, or we can have good control over our destinies, but rarely both.

Negative Possibilities

No one can afford to dwell for long on how fragile and frightening life is. When using a crosswalk, a pedestrian cannot look up at approaching traffic and wonder, "What if the brakes on one of those cars fail?" He must assume the approaching cars' brakes will hold. Yet because we know that things sometimes do go wrong, we live with a twilight awareness of potential accidents, crime, disease, layoffs, betrayals, terrorism, and other threats. We have to tune out our fears because otherwise they would overwhelm us.

But if we completely ignore negative possibilities, problems will catch us unprepared. Finding a balance between being ready for the worst and having healthy optimism is something we have to work at every day. The more information we can handle emotionally, the better we can prepare for problems and the more we can respond appropriately if problems do come up.

Negative Realities

While we must tune out many negative possibilities, it is more problematic when we tune out the negative realities that are already causing harm to us or the people we care about. A woman whose husband drinks more than is healthy may be tempted to ignore a frightening problem or explain it away as "just the way he is" when her husband, herself, and their children would actually benefit from confronting the issue. Some people go the doctor for regular checkups and have their homes inspected by a pest-control company every year. Others prefer

175

not to look actively for problems but to allow them to surface on their own. Of course, ignorance of a medical condition or termite infestation can have disastrous consequences if one waits until there are obvious signs.

Unfortunately, we all learn at an early age that remaining ignorant is an option. Our parents probably steered us away from a good deal of information about the world until they thought we were old enough to handle it. Later in life, we step into that protective role for ourselves, turning away from the realities we find the most troubling.

→ It is worthwhile to identify the areas of your life in which you could actively, constructively seek out more information about potential problems.

→ Facing the truth of existing problems is like jumping into a cold swimming pool. Jumping takes a moment of courage but quickly feels much better than lingering at the edge, dreading the plunge.

Rush to Judgment

As a rule, we are impatient. We skip reading instructions. Long lines at the post office, slow drivers, and even older computers frustrate us. If we have to read a sentence more than once to understand it, we get irritated. When someone speaks slowly, too softly, or with a thick accent, it can be difficult to take it in stride. We want to be there now. We want the world to speed up to our own pace, turn up its volume, adjust its clarity.

Gathering accurate information can be a slow process. The temptation is to draw conclusions quickly so we can move on. Books promising fast solutions (*The Five Minute . . .*) appeal to our desire for expediency. But the world is more plodding than what goes on inside our heads. Television in particular delivers the pleasant suggestion that complex problems can be resolved rapidly with the application of enough cleverness. By being in a hurry to solve problems, we invite frustration and early concession of defeat. When we hurry, we skip seeing facts, and we make poor decisions.

→ Know that the truth cannot always be hurried.

Condensed and Categorized Representations of Truth

Truth cannot always be accurately expressed with an abbreviation. Imagine that a high school student has a chemistry teacher who belittles his students, gives confusing instructions, and devises tests on topics his class does not cover. Suppose his students do poorly in the class as a result. It will not do a student any good to include a note about the bad teacher in a college application. No matter how accurate her descriptions of the chemistry teacher's performance, a college admissions committee member is going to assume the student is just making an excuse for a bad grade. The reviewer has hundreds of applications to sort through and does not want to be bothered with a complicated, possibly false representation. It is much easier to assume the truth is represented by the letter grade, which takes a single second to comprehend.

Other simple representations of information, such as SAT and IQ tests, are similarly easy to accept as representations of truth, although they fail to take significant factors into account. For instance, SATs are timed tests that do not measure long-term perseverance, a factor critical to success in most areas. A person who scores very high on an IQ test might also have significant social problems, making him unemployable in real-life situations. The racial and cultural biases of standardized tests can cause people to underperform. But despite their shortcomings, when condensed representations of truth are available, there is a great temptation to accept them because they are so convenient.

We also condense information whenever we categorize it. By mentally pigeonholing information quickly to make it more understandable, we can distort it. If you meet a man at a party and his appearance and mannerisms remind you of someone else, you may make incorrect assumptions about the stranger. Or if you owned a car that gave you a lot of problems, it might be easy to assume that any car made by that manufacturer would also give you problems. Condensing and categorizing information sacrifices accuracy. We do this all the time, but at best it provides an approximation of the truth, and that limitation should be kept in mind.

Willingness to Gather Information

Working in a large city, I often overhear pieces of conversations as I ride in elevators, wait for walk signals at intersections, and sit at lunch. With surprising frequency, the subject is a complaint, usually about a coworker. While people feel free to vent to their friends, after a few sentences it also becomes clear that the people doing the complaining have never explored their issues with the object of their frustration. By keeping themselves ignorant of why the offender is acting in an irritating manner, or by assuming they already know, they lose any chance to resolve the problem. Maybe they want to avoid a confrontation. Maybe they want to maintain their status as a righteously indignant victim. Or it may be that the complainer has already become so irritated it is impossible for her to approach the offender calmly. Whatever the reason for the lack of communication, the cost of silence is a continuation of the problem. A conversation with the offender might reveal why the other person is being so annoying. From there, it could be possible to negotiate a way around the problem and for the people involved to sympathize with one another. Without exchanging information, all the complainer knows is that she is irritated and convinced she has every right to be.

→ Remember that the courage to gather information, especially from perceived enemies, can go a long way.

The Allure of Familiarity

Sometimes we avoid new information because it interferes with the habits that allow our lives to run predictably. We may resent even the slightest change to a daily routine, such as encountering a detour on the way to work. Being forced into a new circumstance could help us discover, in this example, that the other route is more scenic. We will miss opportunities if we consider unfamiliar options only when they are thrust upon us.

We learn to associate the unfamiliar with the unwelcome. When the unfamiliar shows up unannounced, we are least prepared to appreciate what it has to offer. The engineer who dismisses artists as sloppy dreamers, or the artist who thinks all engineers are tedious, is shutting out a different way of seeing. By welcoming the unknown, we can meet fascinating people and enjoy different restaurants, walks, games, books, films, recipes, hobbies, and all manners of thinking. Otherwise, we end up living in a world more cramped than it needs to be.

Neuroscientists are now encouraging us to seek out novel situations, because those experiences may stimulate our brains and strengthen neural connections. Embracing novelty rather than shunning it may help fend off mental decline as we age.

Thinking in the Short Term

Adjustable-rate home mortgages (ARMs) can offer attractively low initial monthly payments that later can morph into unmanageable obligations. Lenders have historically pushed adjustable-rate over fixed-rate mortgages, while borrowers mentally blocked out the long-term consequences. In 2009–2010, foreclosures rose, and numerous lending institutions collapsed or needed to be bailed out by the federal government. Much of the financial crisis of that time frame can be traced to short-term thinking.

The immediacy of a short-term truth ("This tastes good") can easily overshadow much more serious long-term truths (bacon cheeseburgers are not good for you). Sales pitches encourage consumers' short-term thinking. They capitalize on our desire to believe that the moment can last forever and that small choices will not add up to long-term adverse effects.

→ As important as it is to pay attention to what is true at the moment, you owe it to yourself to pay attention to what is true in the long term.

Visual Illusions We Like Too Much

A construction worker was injured after falling from an attic through a ceiling to the floor below. Normally, a worker at that height would have worn a harness, but this worker did not. Because he was working in the attic area, he could see the sheetrock ceiling below him. He had no reason to expect the ceiling material would arrest his fall from a ladder in the attic. However, the ceiling presented a visual barrier that interfered with his perception and gave him a false sense of security. It was more convenient for him to accept a visual illusion than to deal with a physical reality and put on a safety harness.

In another situation, a commercial building was constructed on an old landfill site. Soil engineers who participated in the design process correctly predicted that while the deep foundation of the building would remain stable, the soil directly under the building would sink over time. Utilities such as the sewer lines, initially laid in the dirt and supported by the earth underneath them, needed to be suspended from the building itself. Some of the contractors did not take this analysis seriously enough, because the dirt under the building had not yet fallen away. It still *looked* solid, so they laid their utilities out on the dirt with insufficient support tied to the building. Sure enough, a couple of years later, the sewer lines began breaking apart as the soil sank away underneath them. Again, it had seemed acceptable to take shortcuts based purely on how things looked, even though the contractors had been warned otherwise.

Our natural tendency to accept general visual appearances is one reason camouflage works. It is also why attractive people tend to get away with bad behavior. According to Alex Kuczynski, author of *Beauty Junkies: Inside Our $15 Billion Obsession with Cosmetic Surgery*, multiple studies have shown that attractive people are treated more leniently by juries.[1] I personally learned about the illusion of physical appearance the hard way. When I was younger, I had a girlfriend who was as cruel as she was beautiful. I had a tough time accepting that such an attractive woman was not a nice person. I tried to weather her stream of belittling remarks, thinking I must have somehow deserved them. It was a long, painful time before I admitted to myself how unattractive her personality was. Visual appearances have a wonderful simplicity, but the conclusions we draw from them are not always accurate.

Boosting Self-Image

We embrace facts that generate or amplify the feelings with which we are most comfortable. We may hang around with people who reinforce a familiar self-image that we like. Our friends may be people who see us as witty, interesting, sexy, or wise. We avoid the people who see us as dull, inept, or unappealing. Yet the people in the second group are in a better position to help us improve; they reflect where we fall short.

Primacy and Recency

We all know that in social situations, first impressions count. When you first meet a person, you have a degree of objectivity about them you will never regain.

Similarly, we are more influenced by the pieces of information received first and last. In a job interview, it is beneficial to be the first or last person interviewed; the ones in the middle have to work harder to stand out. However, in many situations, just because information was presented first or last does not mean it is important. The first and last to be interviewed for a job may not be better candidates than the others; they simply have the advantage of being in the more memorable slots. We need to consciously resist the false importance that can be suggested by random sequences.

I Have Never Had a Sexual Thought in My Life

Just as the founders of this nation created a political template for our society, the Puritans in colonial America created some of its moral templates. The sexual repression of that era has softened over the years, but it has not vanished. In spite of Hollywood's explicitness, in the United States, any given individual is likely to regard his or her sexual behavior as a highly private matter. The need to maintain privacy and avoid shame can cause people to lie about what they think and do. Men hide their impulses. Women learn at an early age that they will be called ugly names if they disclose their passionate side. For many men and women, even small gestures of affection in public make them uncomfortable.

While sexual activity may be discussed openly with third parties in certain subcultures or among close friends, in American society as a whole, it is not. Because we do not freely share the details of our intimate behaviors, an individual's knowledge about sexual behavior is built largely out of personal experience. Except for those in sex therapy, our sexual partners are our only source of information about our skills as lovers. Even between people who are physically intimate, there may be little verbal interchange about sex. Any public discussion is far riskier, posing a danger of being seen as too lusty, or not lusty enough, or even ignorant or perverted. Note how frequently the *Cosmopolitan* article titles listed in chapter 7 incorporate the words *bad*, *naughty*, and *dirty* to frame their topics. While encouraging young women to be sexual, the articles characterize sexual activity as less than completely acceptable behavior. Their titles imply that sex is actually more manageable for readers, if not more alluring, when it is presented as mild deviance.

If a person has sexual impulses he or she does not act upon, that person is experiencing struggles between the impulses (perceived as naughty) and moral sensibilities (perceived as good). Those internal conflicts are an impediment to openly sharing information. It is harder to talk about conflicting feelings than about vehement ones. We prefer to talk about subjects we know we are right about. Disclosing internal conflicts reveals uncertainty, and people do not like to present themselves as uncertain, knowing they may seem weak or indecisive. Besides requiring more work to convey, descriptions of conflict require more patience from the listener.

To deal with our embarrassment when sex is discussed in public, we usually fit the conversation into one of three categories: humorous, dirty, or clinical. But limiting discussion to these three contexts distorts actual experience. To generalize a bit, people do not typically roar with laughter while having sex; they do not exude exaggerated lustiness or recite the breathless, corny lines of pornography; nor, as a rule, do they primly refer to the "penis" and the "vagina." None of the three contexts matches what actually occurs between people during sexual activity. We could talk about sex more frankly in everyday conversation, but we choose not to. The extent to which the lack of free discussion limits our personal knowledge of sexuality is difficult and perhaps impossible to measure. But it is certain that how we limit communication about sex, or refrain from communicating about it at all, obscures the truth. As a result, teenagers may not have the most basic information about avoiding pregnancy and sexually transmitted diseases, and a person in a sexual relationship may not know a great deal about pleasing his partner, because no one ever provided guidance.

An absence of meaningful information also limits what an individual will consider normal and acceptable. If we feel we must hide a feeling, that feeling will seem freakish, as though there is something wrong with it, and with us. The lack of openness and lack of access to information surely cause us to accept things we should not and to miss experiences we need not.

Dreams and Daydreams

Even our private fantasies tend to mislead us. We daydream about what we want but skip over the harder parts, such as actually paying for the Lamborghini or the trip around the world. You may see a man on the sidewalk and imagine having a wonderful romance with him, but in truth, you might only be interested if it turned out if he was not too much trouble. Or you may imagine a stunning flower garden in front of your house, then not want it as much after a few hours of pulling weeds.

An advantage of daydreams is that they allow us to develop a sense of what we deeply desire, which we can then scale back to a realistic, still satisfying goal. I once daydreamed about owning an Austin Healey 3000 sports car. That car was unrealistically expensive for me, but I realized I could afford an MGB. I struggled with the concept that I was settling for less than I wanted, but the stubborn reality was that I could have either the MGB or nothing. When I bought one, instead of feeling I had made a compromise, I found I stopped wishing for a car I could not afford.

A disadvantage of daydreaming is that too much of it can create an unrealistic state of mind. The daydreamer may even start to feel entitled to what he wants because he has spent so much time thinking about it. The desired goal becomes more deeply mentally embedded with each imagining, and as the daydreamer becomes emotionally invested, he may feel deprived of what he imagines. Daydreams can be poisonous in that way.

As for nocturnal dreams, although we know they are not real when we wake up, we *experience* them while asleep. The function of dreams is still not well understood, but we know they can provide us with the illusion of having had actual experiences. The fright or joy in a dream is *real* fright or joy. In much the same way that our moods and outlook are influenced by emotional experiences during the day, emotions accompanying dreams surely shape our moods and outlook as well.

Opinions differ about the usefulness of interpreting dreams. One certainty is that dreams demonstrate that our minds are capable of generating very convincing illusions, even as we simultaneously react to those illusions. We trust our minds not to present us with dreamlike illusions when we are awake, but dreams show that at least when we are asleep, we can project and react to events that did not actually take place. We may react to illusions we have when awake in much the same way.

Fiction and Theater

Historically, fables, myths, and legends have been powerful tools for creating and reinforcing beliefs. Today, films, plays, and novels fill a similar role. The theater has been used for centuries to deliver social commentary and moral messages. We are attracted to stories with linear structure, emotional texture, narrative, and identifiable truths. Interesting characters facing tough challenges draw us into seemingly real worlds. We can discuss fictional characters while driving home from a movie as if they are real people we have just met.

Just as when we pick up a novel and agree to suspend disbelief in order to enjoy the story, we can suspend disbelief when we are offered stories that are not openly revealed as fiction. When returning travelers describe their vacation adventures to us, for example, to make them more interesting they may mix together facts, exaggerations, and outright fiction. We are suckers for good stories, and if we are well entertained, we tend to be more forgiving about lapses of truth. As discussed earlier, advertisers use our love of stories to create scenarios they hope we will buy into.

Although we make a sharp intellectual distinction between fiction and real life, stories can sometimes feel more compelling than reality. Effective storytelling—whether in documentaries, television commercials, political propaganda films, or Hollywood blockbusters—presents intriguing material succinctly, with little or no slack between scenes, and scenes are arranged in an order that point to a conclusion. Because they engage us, the productions can lead us to believe things that are not true. In *Jaws*, film director Steven Spielberg convinced multitudes that sharks are determined to attack humans. But according to the International Shark Attack File kept at the Florida Museum of Natural History in Gainesville, in the 1990s an average of fifteen people died of venomous snake bites every year, whereas the annual number of people killed by sharks in U.S. waters was 0.4.

Filmmakers have always had the ability to create impressions different from reality; the classic movie *Casablanca* was not filmed in exotic Morocco, but in Los Angeles. Today, movies are convincingly realistic even as technological advances allow them to portray such fantastic situations as Los Angeles sliding into the ocean, or human actors inhabiting computer-generated extraterrestrial environments. Fewer limitations are imposed by technology than by the human imagination.

Films not only manipulate scenery but often suggest that our lives could be more interesting. Characters in movies usually have the time and energy to deal with intriguing problems. Except in some art films, the actors do not spend much time trudging back and forth from mind-numbing jobs, going grocery shopping, raking leaves, or calming screaming children. Drabness is simply excluded from movies. This makes for good entertainment, but as with TV, it can have a negative effect on people in the audience if it makes them view their lives as bleak in comparison. Our fascination with movie stars suggests that we have a longing for the improbable lives portrayed in movies. Tabloid journalism reports celebrities' every move, as though stars are tasked with publicly living more interesting lives than the rest of us. It is as if on and off screen, a star must act out a more engaging existence than the ones we know as the audience.

Families of Origin

Within the family unit, children learn ways of handling difficulties. Some families take pains to talk through every interpersonal problem; others deal with conflicts by shouting and slamming doors. When problems are talked through, the truth of cause and effect is emphasized. When doors are slammed, the truth of the accompanying anger is emphasized. Some families deal with problems primarily in a religious context; others pretend the problems are not there at all. Families can be where a child first learns to face difficult truths or where he or she acquires the habit of codependent behavior.

A given family may respond to a new challenge by combining practicality, superstition, and blame. Unlike old family recipes that may be written down, a family's problem-solving methods are acted out and must be adapted to address specific conditions. Even though traditional family problem-solving methods may not even be discussed, they can be passed from parents to children, going virtually unchanged for generations. Conversely, especially as we have evolved from a more rural, agrarian society to one that is more urban, family-based methods for resolving conflicts have become less influential for many. When children grow up and leave home, they may find other problem-solving approaches that work better for them. They also make choices about their careers and marriages and may gradually adopt the belief systems of different religious, political, and social groups, coming to accept truths different from those taught by their families of origin.

The deepest truths of a family are not expressed by its members' religious or political ideologies, but by their actions. A racist family may never sit around listing the reasons they think people of other races are inferior; instead they will shun the other groups and make occasional derogatory remarks. A family that feels shame about an episode in its past may never discuss it at all, and silence becomes its expression.

When family values are not expressed in words but in behaviors, they are harder to identify. Those values are more difficult to challenge because they are not even up for debate. The family values may be meaningfully challenged only through contrasting behavior; the child of a racist family who has managed not to buy into racism herself may be able to express her beliefs, for example, by refusing to laugh at racist jokes and by having friends from other racial groups. A child who declines to go hunting with his father and brothers may be rejecting his family's values more profoundly than an Ivy League undergrad who argues with his family at the dinner table about the virtues of a political party other than the one his family favors. A family member who truly and permanently rejects a family's values and definitions of truth may be teased, disrespected, or ostracized outright. The merits of the dissenter's way of thinking may never be given a chance to come to light.

Truth can also be obscured within families when parents overlook the inevitable flaws in their children. If other adults comment on those flaws, the parents may perceive it as meddling. The net effect encourages children to be ashamed when they begin to recognize their imperfections. Even as adults, we often hide what we believe are our flaws, not just from other people but from ourselves. A myth of perfection initiated by well-meaning parents can discourage children from seeking help when they need it. For a child to acknowledge his or her imperfections might feel like an act of disloyalty to parents with high expectations.

Families interfere with the discovery of truth deliberately as well. A study published in the September 2009 *Journal of Moral Education* showed that 70 percent of respondents to a survey said that lying to children was unacceptable, while an even greater number (80 percent) admitted they had told a lie to a child.[2] Parents lie to control their children's behavior, to spare the child's feelings, to limit the child's perceptions, and to avoid difficult conversations. Clearly, there is material a child cannot handle emotionally. But when lies of omission or commission are told merely for the convenience of the parents, it presents a problem for the child. Particularly if the lying is habitual, the child will eventually realize he or she is routinely being deceived and as a consequence may have difficulty trusting other people as an adult. We appear to agree in principle if not in practice that lies to children should be avoided whenever possible. Most lies are corrosive for everyone involved.

Inarguably, the greatest betrayal is committed in families where sexual abuse is kept secret or denied. If the truth is not brought to light and the child does not receive appropriate help, he or she is at great risk for emotional problems throughout life. The silence of shame has dire consequences for all involved.

Gullibility

We help children enjoy their gullibility. Families find it perfectly acceptable to tell children fantastic myths about Santa Claus, the Easter bunny, and the tooth fairy.[3] Arguably, there are no bad effects, and only a true Grinch would think of taking away such enjoyable experiences.

But children can carry into adulthood the idea that it is fine to perpetuate myths and entertain unrealistic beliefs. This is called "magical thinking." When gullibility persists in adults, it is particularly unfortunate because manipulative people will try to take advantage of it, especially when their targets are at their most vulnerable. Unrealistic hopes can be exploited in innumerable ways, from fake cancer cures, to get-rich-quick schemes, to the false promises of some military recruiters.

As we have seen throughout this book, adult gullibility is also exploited by marketers and political strategists. People can be convinced it is possible to buy their way into the upper class by purchasing evidence of their status. Highly visible items such as expensive cars, watches, jewelry, and clothing are advertised with the implied promise that they will command respect for the purchaser.

People who are not rich can be persuaded they might become rich some day, and that it is wise to vote as though they are already well off. Ordinary people then vote for candidates whose priorities include protecting the interests of the very wealthy. Voting for those candidates helps create the illusion that there is a connection between the ordinary citizens and the upper class. Yet if elected, those candidates push to implement policies favoring elites, policies that necessarily disfavor the ordinary citizens. Because they want so badly to identify with the wealthy, voters can be influenced to lose sight of tremendous economic disparities and what their own interests really are. In 2008, the median household income in the United States was $52,029.[4] As much as we might wish otherwise, most of us are not making millions, but simply earning a living.

There are numerous other ways we do not see our own situations realistically. Most people rate themselves as above-average drivers, making one wonder where all the average and below-average drivers are. You probably know some arrogant people, some impulsive people, some manipulative people, and some mean people, but do you know any people who describe themselves as such? We can develop an unrealistic self-image because we do not get much honest feedback as adults. The opinions of others come freely in childhood when peers make blunt remarks such as "You're selfish!" or "Your ears stick out!" We have to listen harder for criticisms as adults if we are going to learn about ourselves from other people.

Inherited and Childhood Truths

It is difficult to appreciate how much of our general knowledge has been inherited wholesale from our families and school curriculum. While our personal observations in particular situations are unique, we did not invent most of what we know. Just as we can learn thinking and reasoning methods such as mathematics, language, and science, we can learn other systems of thought. These include religions, codes of morality and etiquette, and even how to have fun. We are like hermit crabs that inhabit the abandoned shells of other creatures. Inherited beliefs are extremely convenient, but if we never question them, we inherit their flaws along with their advantages.

While adolescent rebellion can be a time of healthy questioning, some adolescent questioning may not be genuine. Instances of apparent rebellion may be expressions of apprehension about the end of childhood. The adolescent may be painfully aware that soon he or she will have to stop playing and experimenting and instead start living according to a more finite belief system that facilitates an adult existence. That system may include some compromised truths. The teenager senses he or she will no longer be able to mock adult hypocrisy or blurt out the truth. In that way, rebellion may be a final effort to prolong childhood and the honesty that goes with it.

Rationalization and Justification

If we give in to the temptation to cut corners, like a cook who makes too many substitutions in a recipe instead of driving to the grocery store, we either have to admit to ourselves what we are doing or create a distortion of reality to justify it ("I'm just being creative"). Whenever we distort reality with a rationalization or justification, we know that we have played with the definition of truth, confirming just how flexible perceptions of the truth really are. Distortions do not come free; each one we create and each one we see created by others contributes a tiny bit to our intuitive sense of uncertainty about ourselves and the world as a whole.

When people feel cheated, they tend to do more corner-cutting, rationalizing, and justifying. Maybe the cook cuts corners because she resents being stuck with the cooking chores while everyone else watches football. Perhaps she would rather be reading a novel or out walking the dog. The resentment may not be obvious to others; they will just think she is a bad cook. The invisibility of other people's internal rationalizations and justifications is one reason behavior can be so difficult to understand.

→ Make a list of three rationalizations or justifications you allow yourself. Then write down what you can do to make them less necessary. This can be a difficult exercise, but you may be surprised at the result.

Religion

This book would be incomplete without some mention of religious conviction. Religion illustrates our capacity to hold firm beliefs on faith alone. However, religion is a highly personal experience, beyond my expertise and beyond the scope of this book.

To the extent that religious beliefs are a satisfying personal experience, they do not need to be examined here. Two considerations are mentioned because, as with any other system of beliefs, religion can be used to mask important truths:

Abuse. Much in our lives is unclear and uncertain. We are sometimes hungry for guidance, a glimpse of meaning beyond our physical selves or a sense of being part of something larger than ourselves. Some religious leaders take advantage of those desires and use religion to satisfy an agenda, most blatantly by asking followers to donate unreasonable sums of money or through sexual coercion. No religion is immune from exploitation. Fraudulent pitches delivered from inside a religious framework are not always obvious as frauds. No one should hand over money or give up physical or intellectual freedom without first thinking it over very carefully. It is equally important to watch out for and speak up for others who may be less able to protect themselves from abuse.

Fundamentalism. Many people believe that common truths exist among modern as well as ancient religions. Some believe that various religions are different paths to the same destination. While sincere beliefs can be beneficial, they become harmful when those who hold them insist that their religion is necessarily the only valid belief system and that those who hold different beliefs are mistaken. This stance leads to arguments that cannot be won and to wars that last for generations. No one who is genuinely convinced he or she is right about a religious belief should feel the need to prove others' beliefs are wrong.

Afterword: Finding Our Way

The decisions we make are based on many factors, including the availability of objective truth and our experiences, emotions, perceptions, and reasoning abilities. Even when objective truth is available in the form of complete and accurate information, that information is affected by how we interpret it. We have the individual capacity to believe that which is not objectively true, and history shows that the human race has the ability to collectively hold onto supposedly obvious truths that are later proven false.

Without recognizing truths, we have no choices and can only allow things to happen *to* us. The more truths we recognize, the more choices we have, not only about what happens, but about how it happens.

In doing research for this book, I asked many people to share their thoughts, and many generously did so. At times, I also encountered resistance. Understandably, people who faced conflicts were unable to speak freely. Less obviously, some were reluctant to share their private thoughts or shared them but asked me not to repeat them, and I have respected that. I think the occasional reluctance is worth mentioning because it is a reminder that there are beliefs, and no doubt many truths, that people prefer keeping to themselves. They may be among the most valuable.

→ In the preceding chapters we have looked at many sources of information in our lives and at many ways in which we interpret information. But finding the truth in any context is not difficult if we keep some basic principles in mind:

- We tend to think we always need and want truth, but in reality we do not always want it and do not always look for it.

- Uncertainty is uncomfortable; any belief can seem better than no belief. We may adopt the mistaken beliefs of others, indulge in personal mythology, or simply distract ourselves from the uncertainty rather than asking important questions.
- To see more truth, we need to suspect more information exists than is immediately visible, be willing to look for it, obtain the missing information, and be able to interpret it correctly.
- We must remain aware of the dangers of paying attention to the wrong cues, failing to experiment carefully, and believing what we are already inclined to believe.
- Our beliefs are all worth a second look.
- The ongoing task is not only to see truths but to choose wisely when deciding which of them deserve our time and attention.

There are infinite truths to be seen and infinite opportunities to use them to improve our lives.

Notes

For full publishing information, see the bibliography beginning on page 209.

Introduction

1. *Flatow, "Whose Light Bulb?" 10–26.*
2. Charles J. Hanley, "Half of U.S. Believes WMD Claim, Poll Shows," *San Francisco Chronicle,* 7 August 2006.
3. Matthew Kalman, "Al Qaeda Says It Bombed Hotels," *San Francisco Chronicle,* 11 November 2005.
4. *PBS Frontline.* "Rollover: The Hidden History of the SUV," 21 February 2002, http://www.pbs.org/wgbh/pages/frontline/shows/rollover/etc/before.html; Aaron Gold, "New Safety Stats Show SUVs Most Likely to Roll, Cars Least Likely," About.com: Cars, http://cars.about.com/od/safetyfacts/a/roll_results.htm; John Kindelberger and Ana María Eigen, "Younger Drivers and SUV's," National Center for Statistics and Analysis, September 2003, http://www-nrd.nhtsa.dot.gov/Pubs/809-636.pdf; Bailey, "Four SUVs Earn Top Rollover Safety Mark."
5. Maureen Welker, "ICU Psychosis: (Intensive Care Unit Psychosis)," MedicineNet.com, http://www.medicinenet.com/script/main/art.asp?articlekey=7775.
6. Sandeep Jauhar, "When a Stay in Intensive Care Unhinges the Mind," *New York Times,* 8 December 1998.
7. Stephen Colbert used the term *truthiness* satirically, defining it as "truth that comes from the gut, not books." The American Dialect Society voted *truthiness* as the word of the year for 2005, defining it as "the quality of preferring concepts or facts one wishes to be true, rather than concepts or facts known to be true," http://www.americandialect.org/index.php/amerdial/truthiness_voted_2005_word_of_the_year.

Chapter 1: Just Trust Me

1. Mayell, "Bermuda Triangle"; McDonell, "Lost Patrol."

Chapter 2: Eight Types of Lies and What You Can Do About Them

1. Feldman, *Liar in Your Life*; Feldman, "Finding the 'Liar' in All of Us."

Chapter 3: Lessons from Law: Methods for Seeing Truth

1. Kelleher and Merrill, *Perry Mason TV Show Book*.
2. Woods, *Healing Words*; Lindsey Tanner, "New Way to Avoid Malpractice Suits: Just a Simple Apology Can Work Wonders," *San Francisco Chronicle*, 18 November 2004.
3. Henry K. Lee, "Jury Recommends Death For Killings at Meat Plant," *San Francisco Chronicle*, 15 December 2004.
4. Stuart Alexander died in prison of a pulmonary embolism approximately a year later. "Autopsy: Sausage King Died from Natural Causes," CBS5 San Francisco, 19 January 2006, http://cbs5.com/local/sausage.king. Stuart.2.439728.html.
5. Adam Liptak, "Study of Wrongful Convictions Raises Questions Beyond DNA," *New York Times*, 23 July 2007; Innocence Project, http://www.innocenceproject.org/Content/533.php. Note: the Liptak article is also a reference for the discussion of DNA in chapter 6 in a scientific context.
6. Forgas, Laham, and Vargas, "Mood Effects on Eyewitness Memory."
7. Kassin, Ellsworth, and Smith, "Eyewitness Testimony"; Ebbesen and Konecni, "Eyewitness Memory Research"; Ebbesen, "Accuracy of Eyewitness Memory."
8. *NPR All Things Considered*, "Skill-Lay Attorneys"; Pasha, "Last Pitches."

Chapter 4: Thirty-Six Places Where the Truth Hides

1. Tamelander and Zetterling, *Bismarck*; Ballard, Archbold, and Kennedy, *Robert Ballard's Bismarck*; Mark Horan, "With Gallantry and Determination: The Story of the Torpedoing of the Bismarck," KBismarck.com, http://www.kbismarck.com/article2.html; Pacific War Online Encyclopedia, "Swordfish, British Carrier Torpedo Bomber," http://pwencycl.kgbudge.com/S/w/Swordfish.htm (accessed 17 August 2010).
2. Ambrose, "Logging Without Laws."
3. McGee, "Gang Life Is Worthwhile," 154–55.
4. "Gun Regulation and the Second Amendment: Moving Forward After District of Columbia v. Heller," Publication of the Legal Community Against

Violence, October 2008, http://www.lcav.org/pdf/DC_v_Heller_Gun_Regulation_Brochure.pdf; Centers for Disease Control and Prevention, "Surveillance for Violent Deaths."

5. Pollan, *Place of My Own*, 201.
6. Schlosser, *Fast Food Nation*, 193–5.
7. Dennis Gaffney, "Joe DiMaggio: The Hero's Life," PBS.org, http://www.pbs.org/wgbh/amex/dimaggio/peopleevents/pande10.html.
8. Hardy and Nevils, *Ignatius Rising*; Fletcher, *Ken and Thelma*.
9. Department of Defense news briefing, 12 February 2002, http://www.defense.gov/Transcripts/Transcript.aspx?TranscriptID=2636.
10. Haven, *Marvels of Science*, 182; Brown, *Penicillin Man*.
11. Reeve, *Still Me*, 273–6.
12. CaLottery, http://www.calottery.com/Media/Facts/Descriptions/.
13. "Fiscal Year 2006: A Record-Breaking Year for the USPTO," Press Release 06-73, United States Patent and Trademark Office, 22 December 2006, http://www.uspto.gov/news/pr/2006/06-73.jsp.

Chapter 5: Detecting Deception

1. Hansen, "True Lies."
2. Gazzaniga, Gazzaniga, Grafton, and Sinnott-Armstrong, "Brain Scans Go Legal"; Vicki Haddock, "Lies Wide Open," *San Francisco Chronicle*, 6 August 2006.
3. McNichol, "Ultimate Lie Detector," 21.
4. Sean Rosenthal, "The Truth Behind 'Lie to Me,'" *San Francisco Chronicle*, 26 September 2009.
5. Robbins, "Top U.S. Copper Producer."
6. *New Yorker*, 2 November 2009, 23.
7. Anderson, "Consumer Fraud in the United States."

Chapter 6: Lessons from Science

1. *The World Book Encyclopedia*, 2007 ed., 17:192-193; Hurley, *Introduction to Logic*, 42–9.
2. Ibid., 45–9.
3. O'Daly, *Encyclopedia of Life Sciences*, 11:1467–8; see also 1:66–8 re analytical techniques.
4. Gaugh, *Scientific Method in Practice*, 3–6.

5. Centers for Disease Control and Prevention, "Cigarette Smoking Among Adults."

6. Henry Templeman, "Fingerprint Identification Based on Match Probability and Relevant Population," http://henrytempleman.com/madrid_error; "A Review of the FBI's Handling of the Brandon Mayfield Case (Unclassified and Redacted)," Special Report, Office of the Inspector General, March 2006, http://www.justice.gov/oig/special/s0601/exec.pdf; Leyden, "FBI Apology."

7. Adam Liptak, "Study of Wrongful Convictions Raises Questions Beyond DNA," *New York Times*, 23 July 2007.

8. Krivit, *Rebirth of Cold Fusion*, xv; Storms, *Low Energy Nuclear Reaction*, 4–12.

9. Verschuur, *Hidden Attraction*, 125–40.

10. National Institutes of Health, "Iridology: A Systematic Review," U.S. National Library of Medicine, http://www.ncbi.nlm.nih.gov/pubmed/10213874; Stephen Barrett, "Iridology is Nonsense," Quackwatch, http://www.quackwatch.org/01QuackeryRelatedTopics/iridology.html.

11. Elizabeth Fernandez, "Legislators Touched by Leukemia Push to Save Umbilical Cord Blood," *San Francisco Chronicle*, 14 August 2007.

12. Charles Babington, "Stem Cell Bill Gets Bush's First Veto," *Washington Post*, 20 July 2006; John M. Curtis, "Bush Letting Religion Undermine Science," *San Francisco Chronicle*, 25 May 2005.

13. The study focused on "heart failure," defined as loss of the heart's power to pump sufficient oxygen and nutrients throughout the body. Although fish intake did not appear to lower the risk of heart failure, the lead researcher said that there is "strong evidence that [fish intake] protects against myocardial infarction, sudden cardiac death and stroke." J. Marianne Geleijnse, "Intake of Very Long Chain N-3 Fatty Acids from Fish and the Incidence of Heart Failure: The Rotterdam Study," *European Journal of Heart Failure*, August 2009, http://eurjhf.oxfordjournals.org/content/11/10/922.abstract; Reinberg, "Fish Won't Prevent Heart Failure."

14. Robert Stein, "Humans' Arrival Time Gets Another Look," *San Francisco Chronicle*, 18 November 2004.

15. Keay Davidson, "Cosmological Iconoclasts Offer New Ideas," *San Francisco Chronicle*, 15 August 2005.

16. David Vachon, "Universities Won't Hire Albert Einstein," *Old News*, June/July 2007.

17. Nicholas Wade, "Why Chimps Scream During Sex: It's a Bit Complicated," *San Francisco Chronicle,* 18 June 2008.
18. Best, *Damned Lies and Statistics,* 1–8.
19. Huff, *How to Lie with Statistics,* 27–36.

Chapter 7: Media and Misinformation

1. P. Solomon Banda and Ivan Moreno, "Boy Wasn't in Floating Balloon After All," *San Francisco Chronicle,* 16 October 2009.
2. Brian Kates, "Balloon Boy Falcon Heene Throws Up Twice During TV Interviews over 'We Did This for a Show' Comment," *New York Daily News,* 16 October 2009; Mooney, "'We Did It for the Show.'"
3. "Balloon Boy Parents Plead Guilty: Couple Hope to Get Probation in Hoax; Sentencing Next Month," Associated Press, 13 November 2009, http://www.msnbc.msn.com/id/33881293/ns/us_news-crime_and_courts/. Despite his guilty plea, Heene later claimed it had not been a hoax. Ethan Sacks, "'Balloon Boy' Dad Richard Heene Tells Larry King It Wasn't Hoax, Pled Guilty for Wife Mayumi's Sake," *New York Daily News,* 7 January 2010. http://www.nydailynews.com/news/national/2010/01/07/2010-01-07_balloon_boy_dad_richard_heene_now_says_admission_of_guilt_was_full_of_hot_air.html.
4. Society of Professional Journalists, SPJ Code of Ethics, Preamble.
5. McChesney and Nichols, "How to Save Journalism."
6. Public Broadcasting Act of 1967; "Radio Gets In On the Act," adapted 25 March 2005 by Current.org from Jack W. Mitchell, *Listener Supported: The Culture and History of Public Radio* (Westport, CT: Praeger Publishers, 2005), http://www.current.org/history/history0506pba.shtml.
7. "Remarks by the President at White House Correspondents' Association Dinner," transcript, 9 May 2009, http://www.whitehouse.gov/the-press-office/remarks-president-white-house-correspondents-association-dinner-592009.
8. Henry A. Waxman, Remarks to the Federal Trade Commission News Media Workshop, "From Town Criers to Bloggers: How Will Journalism Survive the Internet Age?" 2 December 2009, http://www.ftc.gov/opp/workshops/news/docs/waxman.pdf.
9. Pew Research Center for Excellence in Journalism, "A Study of the News Ecosystem of One American City," 11 January 2010, http://www.journalism.org/analysis_report/how_news_happens.

10. Society of Professional Journalists, SPJ Code of Ethics.
11. Pew Research Center for the People and the Press, "Press Accuracy Rating Hits Two-Decade Low: Public Evaluations of the News Media: 1985–2009," news release, 12 September 2009, http://people-press.org/reports/pdf/543.pdf; http://pewresearch.org/pubs/1341/press-accuracy-rating-hits-two-decade-low.
12. Ibid.
13. Public Policy Polling, "Fox the Most Trusted Name in News?" press release 26 January 2010, http://www.publicpolicypolling.com/pdf/PPP_Release_National_126.pdf.
14. Ahrens, "Accelerating Decline of Newspapers."
15. Cook, "Monitor Shifts from Print."
16. Current and past U.S. Census Bureau information can be found at: http://www.census.gov/compendia/statab/past_years.html, "Information and Communications," U.S. Census Bureau, *Statistical Abstract of the United States: 2007*, Section 24, p. 709, http://www.census.gov/prod/2006pubs/07statab/infocomm.pdf.
17. "Infamous Scribblers: Plagiarism and Fabrication Scandals in Journalism," Freedom Forum First Amendment Center and Diversity Institute Library, http://catalog.freedomforum.org/FFLib/FACLibrary/InfamousScribblers/G-H.html.
18. Matthew Stannard, "New Media Are the Message," *San Francisco Chronicle,* 9 April 2006.
19. Massing, "Now They Tell Us." Judith Miller responded that she had been misquoted: "I did not say that as an investigative reporter, I was not an 'independent intelligence analyst.' I am both an analyst and very independent. What I said was that as an investigative reporter, I could not be an independent intelligence agency." Robert G. Kaiser, James Risen, and Judith Miller, reply by Michael Massing, "'Now They Tell Us': An Exchange," *New York Review of Books,* 25 March 2004, http://www.nybooks.com/articles/archives/2004/mar/25/now-they-tell-us-an-exchange/. Further discussion and information about Judith Miller can be found in: Borjesson, *Feet to the Fire,* 94–7, 244; Michael R. Gordon and Judith Miller, "Threats and Responses: The Iraqis; U.S. Says Hussein Intensifies Quest for A-Bomb Parts," *New York Times,* 8 September 2002.
20. U.S. Census Bureau, "Internet Use in the United States."
21. Nichols and McChesney, "Great American Newspapers."

22. When the material is gossip, its immediate dissemination may help give it more of an aura of importance. Neva Chonin, "Give Us the Gossip and Give It to Us Now! Bloggers Shake Up the Rules, Eliminate the Wait in the Celebrity Gawking Sphere," *San Francisco Chronicle,* 14 August 2006.

23. Pew Research Center, "How News Happens—Still: A Study of the News Ecosystem of Baltimore," 11 January 2010, http://pewresearch.org/pubs/1458/news-changing-media-baltimore.

24. Kirkpatrick, "100 M Videos Each Day."

25. YouTube Fact Sheet, http://www.youtube.com/t/fact_sheet.

26. Carla Marinucci, "Intrigue Grows over 'Hillary' Video," *San Francisco Chronicle,* 20 March 2007.

27. Scheer, "Faked Story About Apple's Jobs."

28. Jessica Clark, "A Singular Sensation: YouTube, MySpace Leading the 'Look at Me' Movement," *San Francisco Chronicle,* 26 November 2006.

29. Shawn Pogatchnik, "Student Hoaxes World's Media with Fake Quote," Associated Press, 11 May 2009, http://abclocal.go.com/wabc/story?section=news/technology&id=6807750; Butterworth, "Web Hoaxes."

30. Andrew Keen, *The Cult of the Amateur.*

31. Verne Kopytoff, "Google Earth Zooms In on Darfur Carnage," *San Francisco Chronicle,* 11 April 2007.

32. Garfield, "Academic Support Student."

33. Patricia Yollin, "The Way We Live," *San Francisco Chronicle,* 15 December 2006, http://www.sfgate.com/cgi-bin/article.cgi?f=/c/a/2006/12/15/CENSUS.TMP.

34. Gandossy, "TV Viewing"; Jones, "Network Television."

35. Henry J. Kaiser Family Foundation, "Parents Say They're Getting Control of Their Children's Exposure to Sex and Violence in the Media—Even Online. But Concerns About Media Remain High, and Most Support Curbs on Television Content," news release, 19 June 2007, http://www.kff.org/entmedia/entmedia061907nr.cfm.

36. Project for Excellence in Journalism, "The State of the News Media 2007: An Annual Report on American Journalism," 2007, http://www.stateofthemedia.org/2007/narrative_radio_audience.asp?cat=2&media=9.

37. Kerr, "Overall Time Spent Online."

38. C. W. Nevius, "A Stupid Radio Stunt's Tragic Finale," *San Francisco Chronicle,* 18 January 2007.

39. Furillo, "Wii Radio Contest."

40. Link to the Lou Dobbs CNN broadcast clip: http://videocafe.crooksandliars.com/heather/lou-dobbs-wants-know-if-his-viewers-would (accessed 5 September 2010).
41. Best, *Damned Lies and Statistics*, 46–47.
42. Magazine Publishers of America, "2008 Circulation Revenue for Top 100 ABC Magazines," http://www.magazine.org/CONSUMER_MARKETING/CIRC_TRENDS/2008ABCcircrevrank.aspx.
43. Leung, "Stephen Glass"; Bissinger, "Shattered Glass."
44. Museum of Hoaxes, "The Hoax Photo Archive: A Catalog of Photo Fakery Throughout History," http://www.museumofhoaxes.com/hoax/photo_database/P30/.
45. American Museum of Photography, "Do You Believe? The Mumler Mystery," http://www.photographymuseum.com/mumler.html; Kaplan, *Case of William Mumler*, 175.
46. Tony Hicks, "Bunk, Junk and Modern Mythology," *Oakland Tribune*, 26 August 2007.
47. Pfanner, "Digitally Altered Photos"; Learning Network, "Doctored Photos."
48. Andrea Thompson, "Fake Photos Alter Real Memories," LiveScience.com, 26 November 2007, http://www.livescience.com/technology/071126-faked-photos.html.
49. U.S. Census Bureau, "Quantity of Books Sold"; U.S. Census Bureau, "Books Sold," 713–14.
50. American Library Association, "Banned and Challenged Books," http://www.ala.org/ala/issuesadvocacy/banned/index.cfm.
51. American Library Association, "First Amendment Basics," http://www.ala.org/ala/aboutala/offices/oif/archive/firstamendment.cfm.
52. American Library Association, "100 Most Frequently Challenged Books of 2009," http://www.ala.org/ala/issuesadvocacy/banned/frequentlychallenged/21stcenturychallenged/2009/index.cfm. For 2000–2009, see the American Library Association site page below, with the Harry Potter series topping the list: http://www.ala.org/ala/issuesadvocacy/banned/frequentlychallenged/challengedbydecade/2000_2009/index.cfm.
53. James, "Pollster Frank Luntz."
54. Solomon, "Questions for Frank Luntz."
55. Frank Luntz, "The Language of Financial Reform," MSNBC.com, January 2010, http://msnbcmedia.msn.com/i/MSNBC/Sections/TVNews/MSNBC%20TV/Maddow/Blog/2010/04/luntz.pdf.

56. Branded Few MC: http://brandedfewmc.com/Branded-Few.htm.

Chapter 8: Lies We Live With

1. Martin, *Iran-Contra Insider*, 4–6; Walsh, *Firewall*, 5–13, 155–6, 230; Zinn, *People's History of the United States*, 585–6.
2. Cannon, "Untruth and Consequences."
3. Snow, "'Death Panels' a Myth."
4. Franken, *Lies and the Lying Liars*, 143–5; Carney, "Frenemies."
5. Swaine, "Hamas Push-Poll Smears"; Cohn, "I Just Got Push-Polled"; Kennedy, "Calls Disparaging Obama"; MacAskill, "Fake Pollsters' Scare Tactics."
6. Frank, *What's the Matter With Kansas?*
7. Mark Martin, "Governor's News-Like Video Brings Backlash / Dems, Labor Leaders See Faults in Release About Workers' Breaks," *San Francisco Chronicle*, 1 March 2005, http://articles.sfgate.com/2005-03-01/bay-area/17363661_1_workforce-development-agency-breaks-labor-unions.
8. Dilanian, "Bridge to Nowhere."
9. Stewart, "Censorship Inquiries 'Rhetorical'"; Snopes.com, "Books Banned by Sarah Palin," http://www.snopes.com/politics/palin/bannedbooks.asp.
10. Whitesides, "Obama's Healthcare Plans."
11. Davis, "Myths Endure on Health Care."
12. Best, *Flavor of the Month*, 1–3.
13. Associated Press, "Taste Test Seems to Confirm That Drinkers Do Enjoy Costly Wine More," *San Francisco Chronicle*, 15 January 2008, http://articles.sfgate.com/2008-01-15/news/17148276_1_three-wines-taste-test-price-comparisons; Rogers, "Price Is Wrong."
14. This person has asked me not to identify him publically.
15. Surowiecki, "Reasonable Panic," 30; Tim Simmers, "Psyched Out," *Oakland Tribune*, 17 November 2006.
16. Ryan Sager, "Money and Your Mind."
17. Randall, "Average Investor"; Brad Barber and Terrance Odean, "Online Investors: Do the Slow Die First?" University of California, Berkeley, Haas School of Business, http://faculty.haas.berkeley.edu/odean/papers/Online/Online%20RFS.pdf.
18. Christopher Shea, "Living in a Hidden-Fee Economy: Things Seem Cheap Until You Tack On the Extra Costs," *San Francisco Chronicle*, 16 July 2006.
19. Pilon, "Fake Amazon Reviews"; Meyer, "Belkin Apology."

20. Culbert, *Beyond Bullsh*t*, 5–8; interview with Samuel Culbert, "The Cure for Common B.S.," *Newsweek*, 7 April 2008.

21. Missouri Attorney General Chris Koster (Web site): http://ago.mo.gov/ConsumerCorner/encyclopedia/rebates.htm.

22. CBC News Marketplace (Canada), "Marketing Rebates: The Science Of 'Slippage,'" 2 January 2005, http://www.cbc.ca/marketplace/pre-2007/files/money/rebates/marketing.html.

23. Grow, "Great Rebate Runaround."

24. James E. Gaskin, "Beating the Rebate Runaround, Part 4: An Insider Shares Rebate Secrets and Offers a Better Way," NetworkWorld.com, 1 March 2004, http://www.networkworld.com/net.worker/columnists/2004/0301gaskin.html?page=1.

25. Consumers Union, "Shoppers Warned That $8 Billion in Gift Cards Went Unredeemed Last Year; Consumer Reports' Survey Shows 27% of Last Year's Gift Cards Still Unused," survey date 18–21 October 2007, http://www.consumersunion.org/pub/core_financial_services/005188.html.

Chapter 9: Advertising: Do You Believe in Magic?

1. Wilmshurst and Mackay, *Fundamentals of Advertising*, 318–9.

2. Ibid., 319–20.

3. Ogilvy, *Confessions of an Advertising Man*, 103.

4. Pratkanis and Aaronson, *Age of Propaganda*, 285–94.

5. Samuel, *Freud on Madison Avenue*, 102; Reichert, *Erotic History of Advertising*, 41. Two best-selling books, Vance Packard's 1957 *Hidden Persuaders* and Wilson Bryan Key's 1974 *Subliminal Seduction*, were also very influential regarding subliminal advertising.

6. Hunter, *Consumer Beware*, 22.

7. Sutherland, *Advertising and the Mind of the Consumer*, 43–54.

8. Whitman, *Ca$hvertising*, 43–54.

9. Twitchell, *Twenty Ads*, 60–2.

10. Arens, *Contemporary Advertising*, 164.

11. Rampton, *Weapons of Mass Deception*, 139.

Chapter 10: Fooling Ourselves

1. Kantrowitz, "Brush with Perfection"; see also Kuczynski, *Beauty Junkies*.

2. Gail D. Heyman, Diem H. Luu, and Kang Lee, "Parenting by Lying," *Journal of Moral Education* 38, no. 3 (September 2009): 353–69. Link to online abstract only, http://www.informaworld.com/smpp/content~db=all~content=a913840594~frm=titlelink?words=lying,children; Bryner, "Parents Lie to Children."
3. Commentary on the everyday reality of the dilemma can be found in Deveny, "Liar, Liar, Parents on Fire."
4. U.S. Census Bureau, http://quickfacts.census.gov/qfd/states/00000.html.

Bibliography

Ahrens, Frank. "The Accelerating Decline of Newspapers: Small Dailies Are Rare Bright Spot in Latest Figures." *Washington Post,* 27 October 2009. http://www.washingtonpost.com/wp-dyn/content/article/2009/10/26/AR2009102603272.html.

Ambrose, Anthony. "Logging Without Laws: Bush's 'Healthy Forests Initiative.'" *Sierra Club Redwood Chapter Newsletter,* December/January 2003. http://redwood.sierraclub.org/articles/December_02/LoggingWOLaws.html.

Anderson, Keith B. "Consumer Fraud in the United States: The Second FTC Survey." *Federal Trade Commission Staff Report,* October 2007. http://ftc.gov/opa/2007/10/fraud.pdf.

Arens, William. *Contemporary Advertising.* New York: McGraw-Hill/Irwin, 2004.

Associated Press. "Student Hoaxes World's Media with Fake Quote." 11 May 2009. *WABC-TV,* New York, NY. http://abclocal.go.com/wabc/story?section=news/technology&id=6807750.

Bailey, David. "Four SUVs Earn Top Rollover Safety Mark in U.S. Test." *Reuters,* March 24, 2009. http://www.reuters.com/article/idUSTRE52N0RP20090324.

Ballard, Robert, Rick Archbold, and Ludovic Kennedy. *Robert Ballard's Bismarck.* Edison, NJ: Chartwell Books, 2007.

Berger, Peter, and Thomas Luckmann. *The Social Construction of Reality.* New York: Anchor, 1967.

Berne, Eric. *Games People Play.* New York: Grove Press, 1967.

Best, Joel. *Damned Lies and Statistics: Untangling Numbers from the Media, Politicians, and Activists.* Berkeley: University of California Press, 2001.

———. *Flavor of the Month.* Berkeley: University of California Press, 2006.

Bissinger, Buzz. "Shattered Glass." *Vanity Fair,* September 1998. http://www.vanityfair.com/magazine/archive/1998/09/bissinger199809.

Bloom, Paul. *How Pleasure Works.* New York: W. W. Norton, 2010.

Borjesson, Kristina, ed. *Feet to the Fire: The Media After 9-11—Top Journalists Speak Out.* Amherst, NY: Prometheus Books, 2005.

Brody, David Eliot, and Arnold R. Brody. *The Science Class You Wish You Had: The Seven Greatest Scientific Discoveries in History and the People Who Made Them.* New York: Berkley, 1997.

Brown, Kevin. *Penicillin Man: Alexander Fleming and the Antibiotic Revolution.* Stroud, UK: Sutton, 2004.

Bryner, Jeanna. "Parents Lie to Children Surprisingly Often." LiveScience.com, 29 September 2009. http://www.livescience.com/culture/090929-parents-lie.html.

Butterworth, Siobhain. "Open Door: The Readers' Editor on Web Hoaxes and the Pitfalls of Quick Journalism." *Guardian*, 4 May 2009. http://www.guardian.co.uk/commentisfree/2009/may/04/journalism-obituaries-shane-fitzgerald.

Cannon, Carl M. "Untruth and Consequences." *The Atlantic*, January/February 2007.

Carney, James. "Frenemies: The McCain-Bush Dance." *Time.com*, 16 July 2008. http://www.time.com/time/politics/article/0,8599,1823695,00.html#ixzz0ynST1dJ7.

Centers for Disease Control and Prevention. "Surveillance for Violent Deaths—National Violent Death Reporting System, 16 states, 2005." *Morbidity and Mortality Weekly Report*, 11 April 2008. http://www.cdc.gov/mmwr/pdf/ss/ss5703.pdf.

———. "Cigarette Smoking Among Adults and Trends in Smoking Cessation—United States, 2008." *Morbidity and Mortality Weekly Report*, 11 November 2009. http://www.cdc.gov/mmwr/preview/mmwrhtml/mm58 44a2.htm.

Cohn, Jonathan. "I Just Got Push-Polled on Obama and Israel." *New Republic*, 15 September 2008. http://www.tnr.com/blog/the-plank/i-just-got-push-polled-obama-and-israel.

Cook, David. "Monitor Shifts from Print to Web-based Strategy." *Christian Science Monitor*, 29 October 2008. http://www.csmonitor.com/USA/2008/1029/p25s01-usgn.html.

Culbert, Samuel A. *Beyond Bullsh*t: Straight-talk at Work.* Stanford, CA: Stanford Business Books, 2008.

Davis, Susan. "NBC Poll: Myths Endure on Health Care, Highlighting Doubts on Overhaul." *Wall Street Journal*, 18 August 2009. http://blogs.wsj.com/washwire/2009/08/18/nbc-poll-myths-endure-on-health-care-highlighting-doubts-on-overhaul/.

Dennett, Daniel. *Consciousness Explained.* New York: Back Bay Books, 1992.

Deveny, Kathleen. "Liar, Liar, Parents on Fire." *Newsweek*, 29 March 2008. http://www.newsweek.com/2008/03/29/liar-liar-parents-on-fire.html.

Dilanian, Ken. "Palin Backed Bridge to Nowhere in 2006." *USA Today*, 1 September 2008. http://www.usatoday.com/news/politics/election2008/2008-08-31-palin-bridge_N.htm.

Dubner, Stephen, and Steven Levitt. *Freakonomics*. New York: HarperCollins, 2005.

Ebbesen, Ebbe B. "Some Thoughts About Generalizing the Role That Confidence Plays in the Accuracy of Eyewitness Memory." University of California—San Diego Department of Psychology, 3 November 2000. http://psy2.ucsd.edu/~eebbesen/confidence.htm.

Ebbesen, Ebbe B., and Vladimir J. Konecni. "Eyewitness Memory Research: Probative v. Prejudicial Value." University of California–San Diego Department of Psychology. http://psy2.ucsd.edu/~eebbesen/prejvprob.html.

Ewin, Stuart. *PR! A Social History of Spin*. New York: Basic Books, 1998.

Feldman, Robert. "Finding the 'Liar' in All of Us." *NPR Talk of the Nation*, 4 August 2009. http://www.npr.org/templates/story/story.php?storyId=111538587.

———. *The Liar in Your Life: The Way to Truthful Relationships*. New York: Hachette, 2009.

Flatow, Ira. "Whose Light Bulb? Edison in a New Light." In *They All Laughed . . . From Light Bulbs to Lasers: The Fascinating Stories Behind the Great Inventions That Have Changed Our Lives*. New York: HarperCollins, 1992.

Fletcher, Joel. *Ken and Thelma: The Story of a Confederacy of Dunces*. Gretna, LA: Pelican Publishing, 2005.

Forgas, Joseph P., Simon M. Laham, and Patrick T. Vargas. "Mood Effects on Eyewitness Memory: Affective Influences on Susceptibility to Misinformation." *Journal of Experimental Social Psychology* 41, no. 6 (November 2005): 574–88.

Frank, Thomas. *What's the Matter with Kansas? How Conservatives Won the Heart of America*. New York: Henry Holt, 2005.

Franken, Al. *Lies and the Lying Liars Who Tell Them: A Fair and Balanced Look at the Right*. New York: Dutton, 2003.

Frankfurt, Harry. *On Bullshit*. Princeton: Princeton University Press, 2005.

———. *On Truth*. New York: Alfred Knopf, 2006.

Freedom Forum First Amendment Center and Diversity Institute Library. "Infamous Scribblers: Plagiarism and Fabrication Scandals in Journalism."

http://catalog.freedomforum.org/FFLib/FACLibrary/InfamousScribblers/
G-H.html.

Friedman, Thomas. *The World Is Flat*. New York: Farrar, Straus & Giroux,
2005.

Furillo, Andy. "Sacramento Jury Awards 16.6 Million for Mom's Death in
Wii Radio Contest." *Sacramento Bee*, 23 August 2010. http://www.sac-
bee.com/2009/10/30/2293355/sacramento-jury-awards-166-million.
html?storylink=lingospot.

Gandossy, Taylor. "TV Viewing at 'All Time High,' Nielsen Says." CNN.com, 24
February 2009. http://www.cnn.com/2009/SHOWBIZ/TV/02/24/us.video.
nielsen/.

Garfield, Leslie Yalof. "The Academic Support Student in the Year 2010," *UMKC
Law Review* 69 (2001): 491.

Gaugh, Hugh G., Jr. *Scientific Method in Practice*. New York: Cambridge University Press, 2003.

Gazzaniga, Michael S., Suzanne I. Gazzaniga, Scott T. Grafton, and Walter P.
Sinnott-Armstrong. "Brain Scans Go Legal." *Scientific American Mind*, December 2006/January 2007.

Gilovich, Thomas. *How We Know What Isn't So: The Fallibility of Human Reason in Everyday Life*. New York: Free Press, 1991.

Gladwell, Malcolm. *Blink*. New York: Little, Brown, 2005.

———. *The Tipping Point*. New York: Little, Brown, 2000.

Glassner, Barry. *The Culture of Fear: Why Americans Are Afraid of the Wrong
Things*, rev. ed. New York: Basic Books, 2010.

Grow, Brian. "The Great Rebate Runaround: Consumers Hate the Hassles and
Hoops. Companies Love Them Unredeemed. Now Regulators Are Wading
In." *Bloomberg Business Week*, 23 November 2005. http://www.business-
week.com/bwdaily/dnflash/nov2005/nf20051123_4158_db016.htm.

Hansen, Mark. "True Lies." *ABA Journal*, October 2009. http://www.abajour-
nal.com/magazine/article/true_lies/.

Hardy, Deborah George, and Rene Pol Nevils. *Ignatius Rising: The Life of John
Kennedy Toole*. Baton Rouge: Louisiana State University Press, 2001.

Haven, Kendall. *Marvels of Science*. Westport, CT: Libraries Unlimited, 1994.

Huff, Darrell. *How to Lie with Statistics*. New York: W. W. Norton, 1954.

Hunter, Beatrice Trum. *Consumer Beware: Your Food and What's Been Done to
It*. New York: Simon & Shuster, 1972.

Hurley, Patrick J. *A Concise Introduction to Logic*, 10th ed. Belmont, CA: Thompson Wadsworth, 2008.

James, Randy. "Pollster Frank Luntz, Warrior with Words." *Time*, 21 September 2009. http://www.time.com/time/nation/article/0,8599,1925066,00.html.

Jones, Elizabeth. "Network Television, Streaming Technologies and the Shifting Television Social Sphere Media in Transition, 6: Stone and Papyrus, Storage and Transmission." The Information School, University of Washington, 26 April 2009. http://web.mit.edu/comm-forum/mit6/papers/Jones.pdf.

Kantrowitz, Barbara. "Brush with Perfection: In a New Book, Alex Kuczynski Explores Our Cosmetic-Surgery Obsession—And Regrets Her Own." *Newsweek*, 30 October 2006. http://www.msnbc.msn.com/id/15362955/wid/11915773.

Kaplan, Louis. *The Strange Case of William Mumler, Spirit Photographer*. Minneapolis: University of Minnesota Press, 2008.

Kassin, Saul, Phoebe Ellsworth, and Vicki Smith. "The 'General Acceptance' of Psychological Research on Eyewitness Testimony: A Survey of the Experts." *American Psychologist* 44 (August 1989): 1089–98. http://www.williams.edu/Psychology/Faculty/Kassin/files/kassin_ellsworth_smith_1989.pdf.

Keen, Andrew. *The Cult of the Amateur: How Blogs, MySpace, YouTube, and the Rest of Today's User-Generated Media Are Destroying Our Economy, Our Culture, and Our Values,* reprint ed. New York: Crown Business, 2008.

Kelleher, Brian, and Diana Merrill. *The Perry Mason TV Show Book: The Complete Story of America's Favorite Television Lawyer, by Two of the Greatest Fans.* New York: St. Martin's Press, 1987.

Kennedy, Kelly. "Jewish Voters Report Calls Disparaging Obama." Huffington Post.com, 15 September 2008. http://www.huffingtonpost.com/2008/09/15/jewish-voters-report-call_n_126694.html.

Kerr, Dana. "Overall Time Spent Online Remains Static." *CNETNews*, 28 July 2009. http://news.cnet.com/8301-1023_3-10297935-93.html.

Kirkpatrick, Marshall. "YouTube Serves 100 M Videos Each Day." Tech Crunch, 17 July 2006. http://techcrunch.com/2006/07/17/youtube-serves-100m-videos-each-day/.

Krivit, Steven B. *The Rebirth of Cold Fusion: Real Science, Real Hope, Real Energy*. Los Angeles: Pacific Oaks Press, 2004.

Kuczynski, Alex. *Beauty Junkies: Inside Our $15 Billion Obsession with Cosmetic Surgery*. New York: Doubleday, 2006.

Lasch, Christopher. *The Culture of Narcissism,* rev. ed. New York: W. W. Norton, 1991.

Learning Network. "Doctored Photos: OK or Not?"*New York Times,* 21 October 2009. http://learning.blogs.nytimes.com/2009/10/21/doctored-photos-ok-or-not/.

Lehrer, Jonah. *How We Decide.* Boston: Houghton Mifflin Harcourt, 2009.

Leung, Rebecca. "Stephen Glass: I Lied for Esteem—60 Minutes: Steve Kroft's Exclusive Interview With Former Reporter." CBSNews.com, 17 August 2003. http://www.cbsnews.com/stories/2003/05/07/60minutes/main552819.shtml.

Leyden, John. "FBI Apology for Madrid Bomb Fingerprint Fiasco." *The Register,* 26 May 2004. http://www.theregister.co.uk/2004/05/26/fbi_madrid_blunder.

MacAskill, Ewan. "Fake Pollsters' Scare Tactics Target Obama." *Guardian,* 3 October 2008. http://www.guardian.co.uk/world/2008/oct/03/uselections2008.barackobama1.

Martin, Al. *The Conspirators: Secrets of an Iran-Contra Insider,* 2nd ed. Pray, MT: National Liberty Press, 2002.

Massing, Michael. "Now They Tell Us." *New York Review of Books,* 26 February 2004. http://www.nybooks.com/articles/archives/2004/feb/26/now-they-tell-us/?page=1.

Mayell, Hillary. "Bermuda Triangle: Behind the Intrigue." *National Geographic News,* updated 15 December 2003. http://news.nationalgeographic.com/news/2002/12/1205_021205_bermudatriangle.html.

McChesney, Robert W., and John Nichols. "How to Save Journalism." *The Nation,* 7 January 2010.

McDonell, Michael. "Lost Patrol." *Naval Aviation News,* June 1973. http://www.history.navy.mil/faqs/faq15-2.htm.

McGee, Albert. "The Gang Life Is Worthwhile." In Charles Cozic, ed., *Gangs: Opposing Viewpoints.* San Diego: Greenhaven Press, 1996.

McNichol, Tom. "The Ultimate Lie Detector." *California Lawyer,* December 2009.

Meyer, David. "Fake Reviews Prompt Belkin Apology." *CNETNews,* 19 January 2009. http://news.cnet.com/8301-1001_3-10145399-92.html.

Mooney, Paula. "'We Did It for the Show.' CNN.com Video of Balloon Boy Falcon Heene." Examiner.com, 16 October 2009. http://www.examiner.com/pop-culture-in-cleveland/we-did-it-for-the-show-cnn-com-video-of-balloon-boy-falcon-heene.

Myers, Greg. *Ad Worlds.* London: Arnold Hodder Headline Group, 1999.

Nassim, Nicholas Taleb. *The Black Swan*. New York: Random House, 2007.

Nichols, John, and Robert W. McChesney. "The Death and Life of Great American Newspapers." *The Nation*, 6 April 2009. http://www.thenation.com/article/death-and-life-great-american-newspapers.

NPR All Things Considered. "Skill-Lay Attorneys Make Final Argument." 16 May 2006. http://www.npr.org/templates/story/story.php?storyId=5409140.

O'Daly, Anne, ed. *Encyclopedia of Life Sciences*, 2nd ed. Tarrytown, NY: Marshall Cavendish, 2004.

Ogilvy, David. *Confessions of an Advertising Man*. New York: Atheneum, 1963.

Pasha, Shaheen. "Skilling, Lay Make Their Last Pitches: Attorneys for the Ex-Enron Ceos Urge Jurors to See Through 'Smoke' and 'Mirrors' of Government's Case. Jury Could Deliberate Wednesday." *CNNMoney.com*, 16 May 2006. http://money.cnn.com/2006/05/16/news/companies/enron/index.htm.

Pfanner, Eric. "A Move to Curb Digitally Altered Photos in Ads." *New York Times*, 27 September 2009. http://www.nytimes.com/2009/09/28/business/media/28brush.html.

Piattelli-Palmarini, Massimo. *Inevitable Illusions: How Mistakes of Reason Rule Our Minds*. Hoboken: John Wiley and Sons, 1996.

Pilon, Mary. "Tracking Down Fake Amazon Reviews." *Wall Street Journal*, 9 July 2009. http://blogs.wsj.com/digits/2009/07/09/tracking-down-fake-amazon-reviews/.

Pollan, Michael. *A Place of My Own: The Education of an Amateur Builder*. New York: Dell, 1998.

Pratkanis, A., and E. Aaronson. *Age of Propaganda: The Everyday Use and Abuse of Persuasion*. New York: Henry Holt, 2001.

Public Broadcasting Act of 1967, as amended, Subpart D—Corporation for Public Broadcasting Sec. 396 [47 U.S.C. 396]. http://www.cpb.org/about-pb/act/text.html.

Rampton, Sheldon. *Weapons of Mass Deception: The Uses of Propaganda in Bush's War on Iraq*. New York: Tarcher/Penguin, 2003.

Randall, David K. "The Average Investor Is His Own Worst Enemy: Terry Odean's Research into Investor Behavior Shows How People Sabotage Themselves." *Forbes*, June 28, 2010. http://www.forbes.com/forbes/2010/0628/investment-guide-behaviorial-finance-odean-average-investor-own-enemy.html.

Reeve, Christopher. *Still Me*. New York: Ballantine Books, 1999.

Reichert, Tom. *The Erotic History of Advertising*. Amherst, NY: Prometheus Books, 2003.

Reinberg, Steven. "Study Finds Fish Won't Prevent Heart Failure." *HealthDay News*, 30 September 2009. http://www.medicinenet.com/script/main/art. asp?articlekey=106094.

Robbins, Ted. "Arizona Is Top U.S. Copper Producer." *NPR Morning Edition*, 16 November 2007. http://www.npr.org/templates/story/story. php?storyId=16349342.

Rogers, Mike. "The Price Is Wrong." *Caltech News* 42, no. 1, 2008. http://pr.caltech.edu/periodicals/CaltechNews/articles/v42/price.html.

Sager, Ryan. "Money and Your Mind: When No News is Good News." Smart Money.com, 1 January 2010. http://www.smartmoney.com/spending/deals/when-no-news-is-good-news/?CID=1260.

Samuel, Lawrence R. *Freud on Madison Avenue: Motivation Research and Subliminal Advertising in America*. Philadelphia: University of Pennsylvania Press, 2010.

Scheer, David. "Teen is Said to Have Faked Story About Apple's Jobs (Update 2)." *Bloomberg*, 24 October 2008. http://www.bloomberg.com/apps/news? pid=newsarchive&sid=ahAlYCNB4qVo.

Schlosser, Eric. *Fast Food Nation: The Dark Side of the All-American Meal*. New York: Harper Perennial, 2002.

Searle, John. *The Construction of Social Reality*. New York: Free Press, 1997.

Smith, Huston. *Forgotten Truth: The Common Vision of the World's Religions*. New York: HarperCollins, 1976.

Snow, Kate. "Health Care 'Death Panels' a Myth: Claims That House Health Care Reform Bill Would Create 'Death Panels' Are Untrue." *ABC News*/Politics. August 10, 2009. http://abcnews.go.com/Politics/story?id=8298267&page=1.

Society of Professional Journalists. SPJ Code of Ethics. http://spj.org/ethic-scode.asp.

Solomon, Deborah. "Questions for Frank Luntz." *New York Times*, 21 May 2009. http://www.nytimes.com/2009/05/24/magazine/24wwln-q4-t.html.

Storms, Edmund. *Science of Low Energy Nuclear Reaction: A Comprehensive Compilation of Evidence and Explanations About Cold Fusion*. Singapore: World Scientific Publishing, 2007.

Stuart, Paul. "Palin: Library Censorship Inquiries 'Rhetorical.'" *Mat-Su Valley Frontiersman*, 18 December 1996. http://www.frontiersman.com/articles/2008/09/06/breaking_news/doc48c1c8a60d6d9379155484.txt.

Surowiecki, James. "Reasonable Panic." *The New Yorker*, 12 March 2007.

Sutherland, Max. *Advertising and the Mind of the Consumer: What Works, What Doesn't, and Why*. St. Leonards, NSW, Australia: Allen & Unwin, 2000.

Sutherland, Max, and Alice K. Sylvester. *Advertising and the Mind of the Consumer*. Sydney, Australia: Allen & Unwin, 2000.

Swaine, Jon. "Barack Obama Victim of Hamas Push-Poll Smears." *Telegraph.co.uk*, 3 October 2008. http://www.telegraph.co.uk/news/worldnews/north america/usa/barackobama/3127353/Barack-Obama-victim-of-Hamas-push-poll-smears.html.

Tamelander, Michael, and Niklas Zetterling. *Bismarck: The Final Days of Germany's Greatest Battleship*. Philadelphia: Casemate, 2009.

Tetlock, Philip. *Expert Political Judgment: How Good Is It? How Can We Know?* Princeton: Princeton University Press, 2005.

Twitchell, James B. *Twenty Ads That Shook the World: The Century's Most Groundbreaking Advertising and How It Changed Us All*. New York: Three Rivers Press, 2000.

U.S. Census Bureau. "Information and Communications." *Statistical Abstract of the United States: 2007*, Section 24. http://www.census.gov/prod/2006pubs/07statab/infocomm.pdf.

———. "Internet Use in the United States: October 2009, Appendix Table A. Households with a Computer and Internet Use: 1984 to 2009." October 2009. http://www.census.gov/population/www/socdemo/computer/2009.html.

———. State and County Quick Facts. http://quickfacts.census.gov/qfd/states/00000.html.

U.S. Patent and Trademark Office. "Fiscal Year 2006: A Record-Breaking Year for the USPTO." Press Release 06-73, 22 December 2006. http://www.uspto.gov/news/pr/2006/06-73.jsp.

Verschuur, Gerrit L. *Hidden Attraction: The History and Mystery of Magnetism*. New York: Oxford University Press, 1996.

Walsh, Lawrence E. *Firewall: The Iran-Contra Conspiracy and Cover-Up*. New York: W. W. Norton, 1998.

Whitesides, John. "Views Unchanged On Obama's Healthcare Plans: Poll." *Reuters*, 19 August 2009. http://www.reuters.com/article/idUSTRE57I01T 20090819.

Whitman, Drew Eric. *Ca$hvertising: How to Use More Than 100 Secrets of Ad Agency Psychology to Make Big Money Selling Anything to Anyone*. Franklin Lakes, NJ: Career Press, 2008.

Wilmshurst, John, and Adrian Mackay. *The Fundamentals of Advertising*, 2nd ed. Burlington, MA: Butterworth-Heinmann, 1999.

Woods, Michael. *Healing Words: The Power of Apology in Medicine*. Oak Park, IL: Doctors in Touch, 2004.

Zimbardo, Philip. *The Lucifer Effect*. New York: Random House, 2007.

Zinn, Howard. *A People's History of the United States, 1492–Present*. New York: Harper Perennial, 2003.

Index

Quest Books

encourages open-minded inquiry into
world religions, philosophy, science, and the arts
in order to understand the wisdom of the ages,
respect the unity of all life, and help people explore
individual spiritual self-transformation.

Its publications are generously supported by
The Kern Foundation,
a trust committed to Theosophical education.

Quest Books is the imprint of
the Theosophical Publishing House,
a division of the Theosophical Society in America.
For information about programs, literature,
on-line study, membership benefits, and international centers,
see www.theosophical.org
or call 800-669-1571 or (outside the U.S.) 630-668-1571.

To order books or a complete Quest catalog,
call 800-669-9425 or (outside the U.S.) 630-665-0130.

About the Author

G. Randy Kasten is a civil-litigation attorney with twenty-five years of experience. He has presided as a judge and acted as an arbitrator, written dozens of legal articles, edited legal newsletters, and given public presentations on legal topics.

Photo by Eliot Khuner

More Praise for G. Randy Kasten's

Just Trust Me

"*Just Trust Me* is a needed resource for finding truth in a world in which we are too accustomed to accepting corporate marketing propaganda as fact. Randy Kasten reveals how the lack of accurate and forthright information is destructive to our health, social institutions, and communities. As a prevention advocate, I appreciate the thorough analysis and strategies presented for navigating and reducing misinformation and distortion in the media. *Just Trust Me* is a valuable tool for advancing community well-being and equity."

—**Larry Cohen**, MSW, Founder and
Executive Director, Prevention Institute

"In *Just Trust Me*, attorney G. Randy Kasten offers a pragmatic and engaging guide to finding the truth in the complex realities of our daily lives. In a voice that is assured, witty, and trustworthy, he provides invaluable tools for sorting out truth from spin, reality from illusion. Highly recommended."

—**Blair Kilpatrick**, Ph.D.,
psychologist and author of *Accordion Dreams*

"Anyone listening to the arguments surrounding healthcare reform should keep a copy of this book in their back pocket. The types of spin Kasten describes are all there, from obfuscation with statistics to misdirection and errors of omission. If you're sick of lies, *Just Trust Me* will be uniquely therapeutic."

—**Douglas Perednia**, M.D., author,
Overhauling America's Healthcare Machine